EVANGELISM IN THE INVENTIVE AGE

EVANGELISM IN THE INVENTIVE AGE

DOUG PAGITT

Abingdon Press
Nashville

EVANGELISM IN THE INVENTIVE AGE
Copyright © 2014 by Doug Pagitt
Reprinted and published by Abingdon Press
First published by Sparkhouse Press

This book is printed on acid-free paper.

Library of Congress Cataloging-in-Publication Data has been requested.

ISBN 978-1-6308-8081-1

14 15 16 17 18 19 20 21 22 23—10 9 8 7 6 5 4 3 2 1
MANUFACTURED IN THE UNITED STATES OF AMERICA

CONTENTS

SECTION 1

I'M AN EVANGELIST

I'm an evangelist. I have been an evangelist since the day I became a Christian, at the age of sixteen.

I grew up in an *intentionally* nonreligious home. There were churches on every corner, but we didn't go to any of them. Ever. On purpose. I didn't know anyone who was interested in Christianity or even religion in general—at least that's what I assumed, since I never heard anyone I knew talk about faith of any kind. When I was sixteen, a buddy invited me to see a performance of the Passion play, and I found myself compelled to give my life to the story I saw that night.

After that, I was eager to share this story with nearly everyone I met, whether they wanted to talk about it or not.

In high school, I spent lunch hour talking to my friends about Christianity, and I wrote about my faith in my classes so I could share my faith with my teachers.

On weekends, my friends and I would drive around Minneapolis–St. Paul looking for groups of "lost" teenagers—skate punks, gang kids, those packs of teenagers who hang out on the street corners waiting for the right adventure to come along—and talk to them about our God.

In college, I spent my spring break walking around Daytona Beach talking to other college students about the meaning of life.

After I graduated, I joined a basketball ministry team that played in cities throughout Central America with the hope of introducing our opponents to Jesus.

As a youth pastor, I led training programs to help teenagers engage in evangelism with their friends and families.

I've led international trips designed to help adults and teens engage in evangelism with strangers.

I've spoken at youth rallies and events where I shared the story of Jesus with hundreds of people at a time.

I started a church with the hope of helping people find the story of God in their lives in real and practical ways.

My evangelistic "philosophy" has changed over the years, but my compulsion to urge others to see God in the world and live in harmony with God has remained.

It is my constant engagement in evangelism in my nearly thirty years of Christian faith that has led me to deeply reconsider many of my assumptions about evangelism.

I haven't just been on the giving end of the evangelistic conversation.

I AM AN EVANGELIST, BUT I AM ALSO EVANGELIZED ON A REGULAR BASIS.

I have the privilege of sharing my life with people who are constantly showing me what God is up to in the world, people who graciously invite me to join them as they figure out how to be part of God's agenda. Some of them are church professionals, some are farmers, some run camps or orphanages or coffee shops. Some are older than I am, some of them are quite a bit younger than I am. Some are dying, some have just been born. And I gladly welcome their invitations.

Because I talk and write about Christianity in ways that sometimes challenge people's ideas about faith and church and community, there are people who feel compelled, even obligated, to contact me by e-mail, voicemail, even U.S. Postal Service mail to tell me I should repent and change my beliefs, my words, and my influence. They're worried that I'm proclaiming news that isn't remotely good.

A few days ago I received a handwritten letter from someone I've never met. This person included a bizarre brochure titled "Shocking Truth—Yahweh Decrees Punishment." It connected natural disasters with dangerous theology like mine.

I also recently received an e-mail with the subject line "A Message of Warning." The e-mail listed several concerns for my eternal well-being and finished with the sentence, "I can only hope that you'll repent, but I hope even more that like Paul, the scales would fall from your eyes, and that you'd see (by the revelation of God the Holy Spirit) the false/heretical 'gospel' that you preach."

I really do pay attention to what these people have to say. If it's possible, I try to have actual conversations with my evangelists by responding to their e-mails, letters, and calls.

I know they are genuinely worried about me and about the people I might influence. I want to stay open to the ideas of others and keep an ear tuned to the prophets among us. But our discussions rarely end with anything but frustration. For both of us.

For me, the problem isn't that they want me to turn away from what they believe to be heresy. It's that they want me to do something that is about as unappealing to me as my ideas are to them. They want me to fear God. And when they start talking like that, well, they might as well be speaking to me in another language. Even in my earliest days of faith, I found the "fear God" approach to be so far from the news of Jesus that I've never given it much consideration. It just doesn't fit with how I understand the story of God.

My evangelists don't always try the fear approach. Sometimes my fellow Christians just want to tweak what I believe. Not long ago, I was at a conference for church leaders. I was standing in the lunch line with a nice Lutheran who wanted me to reconsider my views on baptism and the way we practice baptism at our church. He was concerned that we "not undo the promises of God" by allowing people to practice both infant baptism and what is often called "believers' baptism."

For some reason, I also have a knack for attracting Mormon missionaries. Perhaps it's my willingness to make eye contact as they walk or bicycle by me. These conversations usually end up with them asking me to consider building up my faith by reading the *Book of Mormon* and seeing if I indeed experience a "testimony."

Then there are the folks who want me to convert completely. They want me to change from one faith to another.

Last month, as a result of some growing friendships in Minnesota's Muslim community, I attended an *Iftar* meal with members of a mosque as they broke the Ramadan fast. While I waited in line for the meal, a passionate, winsome young man implored me to consider the value of the five pillars of Islam in my own life and submit to God "more completely."

On another occasion, a dear friend asked me to "consider my inner mystic" so I could become more spiritual.

Even my friend August Birkshire, president of the Minnesota Atheists, assured me that if I would follow his reasoning I could be freed from my "mythical belief systems." He offered me a small card that read "Saved by an Atheist."

It seems a lot of evangelizing is going on, at least around me.

Whether it's me doing the talking or someone else talking to me, I can't help but wonder what it is we're up to. Evangelistic conversations are so odd, so unlike anything else in our lives, that they seem to take on a different cast than other conversations. Whenever I become aware of that oddness, I find myself wondering if evangelism as we know it is working or if it's even appropriate.

I WONDER IF WE SHOULD EVANGELIZE ONE ANOTHER AT ALL.

It seems I'm not the only one wondering about the goodness of evangelism. When I tell people I'm working on a book about evangelism, they have one of three responses:

The chilly response, in which they assume I'm telling them about my book as a means of evangelizing them, and if they show too much interest I'll launch into the Four Spiritual Laws;

The heated response, in which they rattle off a long list of frustrations with the practice of evangelism as they know it;

Or the please-suggest-something-that-will-make-evangelism-okay response, in which people share their hopeful but not overly optimistic desire that there might be a way of sharing the story of God that is respectful and meaningful to everyone involved.

I have yet to meet someone who is neutral on this subject.

CONFORMING OR TRANSFORMING?

I get why we have this impulse to evangelize. And I think it's a wonderful impulse. There's something in us that wants other people to know what we know, love what we love, value what we value, especially when what we know and love and value seems profoundly good. We want to share what we've got.

But I find that evangelism rarely *feels* like sharing something good. In most situations, it feels like an effort to make a person change. When people evangelize me, they don't tell me what they love about their faith; they tell me what's wrong with mine. They don't share what's life-giving or hopeful about what they've found; they warn me about the dangers of continuing down my current path.

For these folks, evangelism is about conformity— conformity to particular ideas, practices, and beliefs. From this perspective, the role of the evangelist is to help people see the wayward path they're on, change course, and become conformed to the likeness of Christ. While this desire to see people change comes out of the best of intentions, I'm convinced that conformity rarely works out the way we want it to. Conformity simply doesn't last. It's like a cast on a broken leg—it might help in the healing for a short time, but if it's left in place, atrophy sets in. Conformity is temporary.

What I find most problematic in this approach to evangelism is that it feels more like conformity than a call to true freedom. In nearly every conversation I have with a person who wants to evangelize me, there is some external model of faith that they want to impose on me, one that doesn't take into account who I am or what I'm about—my hopes, my dreams, my fears, my passions, my struggles. It starts with the answer and my need to get in line with it.

Maybe that approach works temporarily for people who are truly unhappy or confused about their lives. And maybe they even concede for a while and try to live out whatever story of faith they've been handed. But in the long run, it doesn't stick. There is a natural bent, an inner narrative, a life force in each of us that wants to shine through.

WHEN AN EVANGELISTIC MESSAGE IS NOT IN HARMONY WITH THAT NARRATIVE, IT'S SIMPLY NOT SUSTAINABLE.

Those of us who evangelize are truly hoping for a better result. When we proclaim good news, we hope that news finds a home in the hearts and minds of the people who hear and witness our proclamations. We want it to resonate with them in that deep, profound way that only the truest things can do.

I want the good news I proclaim to ring true and weave its way into the roots of someone's story. That's how the good news becomes more than the cast that holds a broken life together. It becomes the new growth, the new bone that heals and strengthens not only what's broken, but everything that surrounds it.

SO MY GUIDING IDEA OF EVANGELISM IS NOT CHANGE.

It's not conversion.

It's resonance.

At the heart of my suggestions for evangelism in the Inventive Age is my belief that all people are created in the image of God and have within themselves aspects of God. Each of us has core passions and fears, and when our core passions are met by God's actions, we resonate with good news.

I'm not only saying this is how it ought to be, I'm suggesting that this is the way it always has been. Any evangelistic engagement that might be deemed "success-ful" turned out that way because the story we were telling connected with the core passion or fear in the person. And because there are at least nine differing core passions and fears—we will talk about these more later—any single approach is only successful for some people, some of the time. An approach that might be deeply meaningful to some people can be completely uninteresting to others. I don't think that's due to a lack of something in the evangelist or the prospective convert. I think it's because the story we are telling is too big to be confined to a one-size-fits-all method of conversion. What's good news for one person might not be good news for someone else.

PROCLAIMING GOOD NEWS

Wikipedia, the popular Internet encyclopedia, says evangelism is "the practice of relaying information about a particular set of beliefs to others who do not hold those beliefs." This seems to be a common view of evangelism.

I wish it weren't.

I don't think that definition captures the beauty, intimacy, and power of real evangelism. The way I see it, evangelism is not simply relaying information. It is far more invitational. It's not about changing beliefs. It is about actively entering into an ongoing, life-giving story with one's entire life.

In the process of putting together this book, I've been more aware than ever of just how much work is involved in reclaiming this vision of evangelism.

For example, I am privileged to have a number of really smart, theologically minded, and sometimes-funny friends on Facebook. As part of my research, I threw out some questions to the Facebook universe to see what I'd learn. I started with a status update that said, "How do you define evangelism?"

Within thirty minutes, I had the following responses, showing the mixed feelings on the subject:

Adam Walker Cleaveland: Evangelism is bearing witness to what God has done, is doing, and will do in the world and in one's life, engaging others in Spirit-dialogue and inviting people to faith.

Gene Ramsey: Evangelism is sharing the good news of the gospel in such a way that it is given an opportunity to actually be heard.

James Hunt: Evangelism: initiating others into the Reign of God. (thanks, Elaine Heath)

Lisa Boylan: Living my life—honestly, peacefully and with love. I'm horrid at verbally proclaiming something and it often bothered me (in the past) that I didn't feel comfy "talking" to others in a more bold manner. I've grown to realize that my personal journey is the way I evangelize. Many people have asked me about Christ because of that very thing . . . which I'm thrilled about—just don't get me jabbering on and on 'cause I'll flub it up.

Josh Blanchard: Evangelism is best done and defined as the community of faith witnessing to the good news that the kingdom of God is upon us.

Lisa Boylan: SEE! I can't even form a clear, concise answer! Sheesh.

Andy Wade: Shedding the light of Christ on the mysteries of God and inviting others to join the journey.

John Martinez: Evangelism is annoying my neighbors with the premise that I am somehow better than they are and that they can be like me if they just listen to me, because I am that good, and therefore better than them.

Krzysztof Raczkowiak: Evangelists say, "All men are equal, but we are more equal than others."

Nathan Willard: Evangelism is simply sharing the good news concerning what Jesus, God the Son, did and is doing to reclaim and restore humans and the world. If we make it about what we are doing, then it can easily become: "I'm better than you." When we keep the focus on Jesus and what he did, it remains about how we were all in rebellion against God and in need of reconciliation.

Pamela Chaddock: The invitation that welcomes everyone into the Family of God.

Tim Lyles: I define evangelism as the same thing that those 4 good news books do [you know, Matty, Marcus, Lucas and JohnnyB] . . . tell the Jesus story in a way that makes sense to a particular audience and get outda way and let Spirit God do some heart transforming. It doesn't hurt to read that Isaiah scroll thing either.

If my Facebook friends are an indication, there's little consensus on the nature of evangelism. I think that's because we all sense that there ought to be something better than the evangelistic approach we've been taught and subjected to.

In spite of the baggage people bring to their ideas about evangelism, there seems to be a common thread in our collective understanding of this practice. At its heart, evangelism is about telling something, sharing something, offering something.

The word *evangelism* came into the Christian vocabulary from Koine Greek, the language used in the writing of the New Testament. The Koine (or common) Greek word used in the original text was εὐαγγέλιον, which referred to good tidings and the reward given to the messenger who delivers this good news.

This helps explain why the same word is also the source of the English word *angel*. Angels in the Bible didn't just float around and keep an eye on things. Almost every time they show up in the biblical narratives, they are there to proclaim good news. Think of the angel coming to the shepherds in Luke's narrative of the birth of Jesus: "Don't be afraid! Look! I bring good news to you— wonderful, joyous news for all people."[1]

Evangelism, it seems, has little to do with the person doing the evangelizing and everything to do with the message itself. It's the content—the goodness of the news to the hearer—that makes it noteworthy in the Bible, not the delivery device.

The prophet Isaiah uses this notion of evangelism to speak of those who declare the good news of God: "How beautiful upon the mountains are the feet of a messenger who proclaims peace, who brings good news, who proclaims salvation, who says to Zion, 'Your God rules!'"[2]

The four New Testament Gospels are named for the four evangelists and use the same word, εὐαγγέλιον, for *evangelist*. The title evangelist was given to those who were doing much more than conveying facts. They were engaging in the complex act of telling the story of how God was at work in the world through Jesus and his followers. This story was being told both to those who had never heard it and to those who had heard it many times. Evangelism was about a desired message, the good news, not about facts that demanded assent. The Gospels are not a dry transcription of every word, but a living act of heralding the story of God.

EVANGELISM IS NOT THE ACT OF TELLING; IT IS THE ACT OF COMMUNICATING.

This implicates the messenger and the hearer. Luke the Evangelist begins his Gospel by saying:

> Many people have already applied themselves to the task of compiling an account of the events that have been fulfilled among us. They used what the original eyewitnesses and servants of the word handed down to us. Now, after having investigated everything carefully from the beginning, I have also decided to write a carefully ordered account for you, most honorable Theophilus. I want you to have confidence in the soundness of the instruction you have received.[3]

The Gospel is addressed to Theophilus. Some suggest this was a single person, while others argue that Theophilus represented a group of Greek-speaking people the way people use "Dick and Jane" to represent anyone and everyone. Either understanding of Theophilus leaves us knowing that the Gospel of Luke was not a list of impersonal facts being distributed to a wide audience. It was a thoughtfully crafted narrative meant to help a particular group of people know that they could trust the story they were living.

Each Gospel is a message of personal engagement where the news is not only proclaimed but heard. The goodness of the news needs to be received on both sides of the engagement.

The Gospel of John the Evangelist adds a little punch to this proclamation. John writes, "Then Jesus did many other miraculous signs in his disciples' presence, signs that aren't recorded in this scroll. But these things are written so that you will believe that Jesus is the Christ, God's Son, and that believing, you will have life in his name."[4]

John the Evangelist makes the point that the good news he's proclaiming is only part of the story, that there is more to tell. It's an invitation to join in with the story and see where it leads. Like Luke, John tailors his telling to a particular group of people—the "you" in 20:31. Theologians have spent lots of time and energy debating whom the "you" might be, but regardless of the answer, it's clear this message was intended for someone.

THE GOSPEL IS ALWAYS AN INTIMATE MESSAGE OF GOODNESS.

EVANGELISM AS RESONANCE

The concept of resonance is fascinating. It's found in all kinds of fields—electronics, astronomy, quantum mechanics, music, engineering—and the geek in me can't read enough about it. In its simplest terms, resonance is based on the idea that everything has a frequency— vibrations of energy it emits. Resonance occurs when those vibrations meet up with other vibrations operating on the same frequency. When that happens, there's a transfer of energy from one source of energy to the other source.

Take verbal communication, for example. Your vocal cords create a vibration at a frequency that is picked up by the ears of the person you're talking to. Her brain makes sense of those vibrations and connects them with words she's learned. You speak and she hears, because of the transfer of energy between your voice and her ears.

But that transfer isn't enough to create resonance. Resonance happens when two sources of energy share the same frequency. The classic example involves tuning forks, those funny little metal forks you hit to get a particular musical pitch. Every tuning fork gives off a particular frequency. Scientists have found that if you take two identical tuning forks, mount each on a wooden box, then strike one of the forks to make it ring out its note, the other, un-struck tuning fork will start to ring as well. There is a transfer of energy between the two tuning forks that happens only because they share the same frequency. That phenomenon is called resonance.

We witness resonance all the time. It's the reason a pendulum sways, the reason moons orbit other planets. It's why playground swings move the way they do and what holds suspension bridges together. It's why your inner ear works the way it does and why tides change with the phases of the moon.

I don't want to get all Carl Sagan here, but everything in all of creation is vibrating. All matter that we experience as solid is made stable by vibrations. Every cell, every particle, every light and sound wave is vibrating. The entire cosmos is singing with vibration. That's why I think vibration, frequency, and resonance are great ways to describe the engagement of human beings with God.

When an idea or a person or an experience hits us deep in our center, we say it resonates with us. Something about that idea or person or experience has struck the frequency of our lives just right. And when that happens, we vibrate with the same energy as that tuning fork. These resonating experiences are far more than the words we say; they are the actions in which we engage.

So if we are going to be people who proclaim good news to the world, we'd better make sure that good news resonates with someone.

WHEN GOD'S STORY RINGS TRUE, THAT'S WHEN CONVERSION HAPPENS.

That's when we are released from our fears and made truly free.

I believe that each of us is created in the image of God, that each of us bears the mark of God. We all have a God-given frequency that's humming along in us from the beginning. It seems to me, then, that the task for us evangelists is not to push for outward conformity but to look for the unique frequency in each of us.

I also believe that God is active in the world right here and now. There is a God vibration that runs through everything God created. It is this vibration that runs throughout God's story. Evangelism in the Inventive Age demands that we deliver the good news of God by finding the resonance between God's story and the story playing out in each of us. This is what the first evangelists did when they wrote their Gospel proclamations. It's what we are called to do today.

If you're willing to follow this thread for the next couple of hours, I think you'll start to see that there's something to the idea of resonance evangelism.

But before I move on, I'd like to tell you more about what I see as the fourth "age" in Western culture. I call it the Inventive Age. This cultural shift affects all of society, including religious life and certainly evangelism. In the Inventive Age, we are no longer willing to accept generic fixes for our problems. We aren't interested in having ideas or solutions or dreams handed to us by people who think they have more power or knowledge or influence than we do. The Inventive Age is a time of organic connection, of global wisdom, of shared authority. If we want to practice evangelism in this age, we have to recognize that it doesn't work to tell people to conform to some idea of faith.

WE HAVE TO PROCLAIM A FAITH THAT RESONATES.

SECTION 2

THE INVENTIVE AGE

If you've come to this book having read the other books in this series: *Church in the Inventive Age, Preaching in the Inventive Age,* and *Community in the Inventive Age,* then you already know what I mean by "Inventive Age." If you're new to the phrase, here's a quick overview.

For most of human history, changes in broad social structures came only occasionally and were limited in geographic scope. But in the last two centuries, cultural change has become far-reaching, constant, and increasingly rapid.

In the last two hundred years, American culture has moved through three distinct ages—the Agrarian Age, the Industrial Age, and the Information Age—and now is heavily engaged in a fourth—an era I have dubbed the Inventive Age. With each of these ages has come a shift in what we think, what we value, what we do, and how we do it.

I was once in a small-group meeting with the famed organizational expert Peter Drucker. Of everything he said at that meeting, one thought has stuck with me more than anything else. He said, "The world my parents were born into was essentially the same as the world of Abraham and Sarah from the Bible."

He was right. Drucker, born in Vienna in 1909, was pointing out that the world into which his parents were born—specifically, Austria in the nineteenth century—operated under a social structure that had been in place in rural areas for a millennium. He contrasted that with the world into which he was born—Austria at the dawn of the Industrial Revolution. Just one generation earlier, the majority of human beings lived pretty much as their parents, grandparents, and great-grandparents had. They worked the land, rarely lived more than one hundred miles from where they were born, and knew they'd be lucky to see their fiftieth birthdays. Mid-nineteenth-century culture was, as Drucker said, nearly identical to the culture of the ancient Israelites. Both were part of the Agrarian Age.

The Industrial Revolution of the late 1800s brought about dramatic cultural upheaval in Europe and the United States. Certainly earlier inventions like the printing press had a broad impact on society. But the printing press didn't directly change the way people fed themselves or moved from place to place or earned a living. The Industrial Revolution did.

People moved from farms to cities. Men and women who had once worked alongside one another in the fields left their families at home to work in factories. Manufactured goods became the currency of the culture.

The next cultural shift began while the Industrial Age was still booming. During the 1920s and '30s, the Information Age began to take hold, thanks in no small part to the growth of the manufacturing and shipping industries that had taken place during the Industrial Age. As people had access to books, newspapers, radios, and eventually televisions, knowledge and information became the most valuable assets of the culture.

In the same way, the Inventive Age is being born out of the Information Age. Knowledge is no longer the goal but the *means* by which we accomplish new, even unimagined, goals.

Few cultural institutions have been able to move through all these shifts with their central identity intact. The church has been a steady—though not unchanged—presence in each age. It has remained when so many other cultural institutions have either fallen away completely or morphed so much that they no longer resemble their former selves.

I believe that's because the church has been both shaped by and a shaper of culture.

Some people hate the idea that the culture impacts the church. They like to think of the church as a bastion of stability in a sea of turmoil. They want to believe that the church has somehow maintained a pristine, untouched essence, even as the muck of society has swirled around it.

That's simply not the case.

This isn't an insult to the church. The church ought to place itself squarely in the midst of culture. Everything, from the kinds of buildings we call churches to the way we expect our pastors to preach, our theology to be laid out, and our furniture to be arranged, is meant to communicate something to the culture in which a church functions. I think that's good news.

As American society has moved from the Agrarian Age through the Industrial Age into the Information Age and now on to the Inventive Age, the church has moved right along with it. In each age, the church has adopted new values (the small, rural communities of the Agrarian Age gave birth to the parish model of church), new beliefs (the growing literacy of the Industrial Age changed beliefs about who could and should read the Bible), new aesthetics (the Information Age gave us education wings and Sunday school curriculum), and new tools (microphones and song lyrics on the big screen are products of the Inventive Age) that reflect the changes in the culture in which it exists.

Here we are in the thick of the Inventive Age. It's an age when we have no idea what's coming next or where it will come from—and for many of us, that's thrilling.

Much of what we knew for certain fifteen, even ten years ago—that you needed a cable coming into your house to make phone calls, that a car could only run on gasoline or maybe diesel fuel, that once you started wearing glasses you had to wear them for life—has been turned upside down.

Right now, we live in a world filled with ideas and tools and discoveries we couldn't have imagined twenty years ago. Bioengineered corn is grown in the African desert. You can carry a library's worth of books in your hand and your entire CD collection in your pocket. Scientists can create entirely new materials at the subatomic level. You can get a college degree from your living room. People are living in the International Space Station—and I can talk to them through my Twitter account!

In 1963 the U.S. Patent and Trademark Office processed 90,982 applications. In 2008 it processed 485,312. While the U.S. population doubled in that time, patent applications increased more than five times.

But the Inventive Age isn't solely about inventions any more than the Agrarian Age was solely about farming. As in the previous ages, the Inventive Age is marked by changes in the way we think, what we value, what we do, and how we do it.

In every sphere of society—the hard sciences, social sciences, art, sports, music, health, technology, economics, transportation, communication—the Inventive Age is marked by a level of creativity that surpasses even the Industrial Age for its impact on the culture.

That creativity has altered the way we think about ourselves. Children, young adults, and even older folks no longer wonder what they will be when they grow up. Now we ask, "What do I want to do with my life? How do I want to spend my time? What can I contribute?" These aren't questions about vocation. They are questions about impact, about meaning. We sense that there is no end to the options and that the future is ours to make.

The Inventive Age is one in which inclusion, participation, collaboration, and beauty are essential values. The values of the previous ages still exist, but in different, even subservient, roles. Knowledge is important, but only as a means to discovering something else. Repeatability matters, but only as it relates to advancing an idea. Survival, however, is barely on the radar of most Americans. Where nature was once a major threat, it is now something we have tamed and used and manipulated so heavily that there are cultural movements designed to save it.

Not long ago, humanity feared the earth. Now we fear for the earth.

This is the age of Pandora, where I tell an online radio station what to play. It is the age of the app store, where a major corporation hands control over to an open-source network of ordinary people. It is the age of Wikipedia, where anyone can decide what a word or concept or cultural touchstone means. It is the age when a bunch of college kids create a social network and seven years later it has more than five hundred million users.

IT IS THE AGE OF OWNERSHIP AND CUSTOMIZATION AND USER-CREATED CONTENT.

The impetus behind all of this personalization is not narcissism. It's the longing to attach meaning to experiences. People in the Inventive Age are looking for a sense of ownership, not of things or even ideas, but of our lives. We are keenly aware of our global community and how interconnected *our lives* are with the lives of people all over the world.

That sense of global community can be overwhelming. We want both to create our own place in that community and to contribute to its vitality. We don't want to simply use resources created by and controlled by others. As a result, there is a shift in the seat of authority. It isn't in the wisdom of the village leaders or the deep pockets of the factory owners or the knowledge of the corporate executives. Authority is found in the way our experiences come together and create reality. It is found in relationships. We tend to be suspicious of objectivity, uncertain if it is possible or even desirable. Instead, we give great credence to authenticity, to context. Authority—as much as anything else in the Inventive Age—is user generated.

The implications for the church are just beginning to emerge. In the last ten years or so, the values of the Inventive Age—the drive to create, the search for meaning, the sense of ownership, the open-source mentality that pushes the Inventive Age ever faster into the future—have scattered across the landscape of American Christianity like seeds in the wind.

How they will take root remains to be seen. What is clear is that just as the previous ages created the norms of the church in their day, so it will be in the Inventive Age. And just as church leaders in those ages asked difficult questions about change, it will be up to *you* to decide how you will be the church in this age.

It's far too early to know where all of this will lead— churches all over the world are experimenting with being the church in the Inventive Age, and there's no telling what will take hold and what won't. To be sure, churches in the Inventive Age will have our share of mistaken notions, questionable practices, and bad ideas. But right now, at the dawning of a new age, it all feels like a beautiful revolution.

SECTION 3

EVANGELISM IN THE INVENTIVE AGE

As we move further into the Inventive Age, it's becoming increasingly clear that the changes in the ways we think, what we value, our common aesthetics, and accepted tools have profound implications for evangelism.

The Inventive Age is bringing about changes in the language we use to talk about our faith—the language of the parish church takes on new meaning when the parish is defined by common goals instead of geography. It is changing our sense of purpose—our access to information makes it almost impossible for an Inventive Age church to ignore issues such as global poverty or human trafficking. It is changing the way we gather as faith communities—can you imagine such a thing as an Internet church in 1953? And it is changing how we communicate our message—find me a church without a website and I'll show you a church that's struggling to connect with Inventive Age people.

All these changes in our thinking, values, aesthetics, and tools are changing the way we think about evangelism in the Inventive Age as well. Take our language, for example. By some estimates, in the 1600s—the time of Shakespeare and the King James Bible—there were around seventy thousand words in the English language. In 1990 there were three hundred thousand. Today there are more than one million—and counting.

According to the Global Language Monitor, the English language passed the million-word threshold on June 10, 2009, at 10:22 a.m. (GMT)—with a perfectly Inventive Age addition: Web 2.0.[5]

Our changing language reflects our changing values, which influence the tools we use to live out those values and the aesthetics by which we express them. It's a constant cycle of cultural change. And those of us who want good news to resonate with people living in the Inventive Age need to pay attention to these changes.

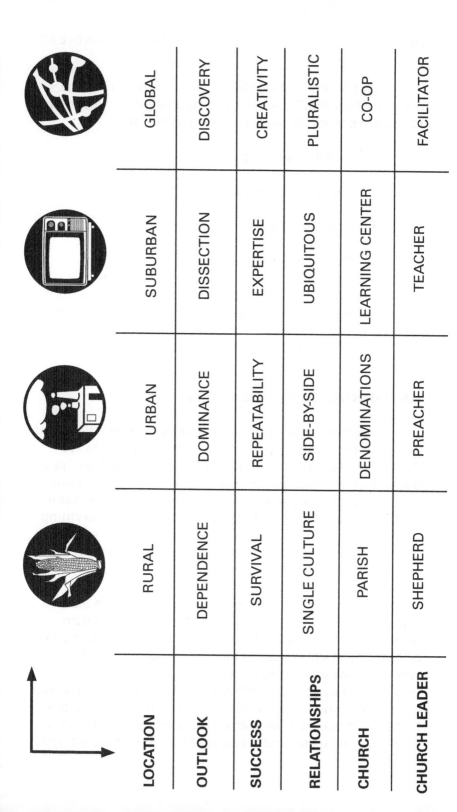

LOCATION	RURAL	URBAN	SUBURBAN	GLOBAL
OUTLOOK	DEPENDENCE	DOMINANCE	DISSECTION	DISCOVERY
SUCCESS	SURVIVAL	REPEATABILITY	EXPERTISE	CREATIVITY
RELATIONSHIPS	SINGLE CULTURE	SIDE-BY-SIDE	UBIQUITOUS	PLURALISTIC
CHURCH	PARISH	DENOMINATIONS	LEARNING CENTER	CO-OP
CHURCH LEADER	SHEPHERD	PREACHER	TEACHER	FACILITATOR

Of the many characteristics of the Inventive Age, there are four that I believe have significant implications for how we think about evangelism in our day:

- An educated population

- The web of authority

- A post-tradition perspective

- Particularity of people

We proclaim the gospel in real time. We communicate good news to real people in real places. That means these cultural realities influence both how we tell the good news and what we determine to be good news.

AN EDUCATED POPULATION

We tend to think of education as its own little world. We know that education helps us, but we don't always think about the ways in which changes in education ripple out into other areas of our lives. But ever since the Information Age that arose in the 1920s, the church has taken all kinds of cues from the world of education—everything from adding education wings to our churches to starting up publishing houses that focus on developing Sunday school curriculum.

The carryover from the world of education also brought with it certain assumptions about evangelism. Back in the 1940s and '50s there was a great emphasis on bringing God's message to the uneducated parts of the world, places where people couldn't read or write. For people who lived out a faith centered on the written words of the Bible, the illiteracy of the rest of the world created huge challenges. So we started translating the Bible into other languages so that those who could read would have something to share with their uneducated communities. Evangelism happened through education. We built schools in African villages and sent our missionaries overseas to teach in them. We took it upon ourselves to educate the world—teach people to read, then the Bible will make sense. And it worked!

Now, for the first time in human history, religion is being practiced by literate cultures.

Religion changed the way we understood literacy.

NOW, LITERACY IS CHANGING THE WAY WE UNDERSTAND RELIGION.

Literacy and religion have always done an odd sort of dance. The church structure that has existed for two thousand years was built on the assumption that the educated clergy had access to information that the masses did not. For many years, the preacher was the most educated person in the community. He was the one who went away to college and returned with the knowledge reserved for the learned. The priest read the Bible aloud and told his listeners what to make of it. His ability to read gave the priest the highest authority in the church. Who else could figure out what God wanted but the one who could read God's Word?

But now most everyone can read the Bible for themselves. We don't need—or want—one person interpreting it for the whole community. Instead, we see ourselves as not only able but required to read the Bible for ourselves and work out its implications in our lives.

AUTHORITY IS NO LONGER AUTOMATICALLY GIVEN TO THE PERSON WHO KNOWS THE MOST.

And people of the Inventive Age have come to believe that reading the Bible is only part of how we work out our faith. We value the "education" we receive in a church setting, but we also value the education that comes from living in the world—traveling, having conversations, taking risks, meeting new people, serving others, discovering new places and ideas. Information has taken a backseat to experience.

The increase in literacy and the heightened value of experiences over information mean that Inventive Age people see ourselves as equals with the official representatives of Christianity. We believe we are well equipped to disagree with the ideas and teachings of Christianity. So it's no longer sufficient—and it probably never was—to treat evangelism as the passing on of information.

As our thinking and our values have changed, our tools have changed along with them. That includes the Bible. As much as we might like to think the Bible is constant and unchanging, the fact is that it has always been adapted to meet the needs of the age in which it is used.

One hundred years ago, a family might have had one Bible in the house—most likely a gigantic hardbound King James Version that was read out loud at family gatherings. Now Bibles are everywhere. Right now I have three different Bible apps on my iPhone. I can access 25 English translations and another 142 versions in 44 other languages, all with a few flicks of my thumb. If I'm not sure what to make of something I read in one of those Bibles, a few more clicks and I can access the best biblical scholarship available. And the beautiful part is that everyone else can too.

Not only can we access the Bible and commentaries and all kinds of information about Christianity, we can do the same for every belief system on the planet. In minutes, we can get information on other world religions. We can read stories about people living out other faiths in ways that seem life giving and beautiful. Where once it was easy to talk about the heathens on the other side of the world, people we would never know or see, we now live side by side with Muslims and Buddhists and atheists. "They" aren't unknown anymore.

And we can find more than enough information about all the wrongs committed in the name of God. We see pictures of dead Christians in Egypt. We read about fringe religious groups boycotting the funerals of soldiers. We see the ugliness that too often comes along with religion.

For evangelists, this unprecedented access to information carries with it endless ramifications. We can't just pass out a booklet, or preach a sermon, or put together a website that tells people Christianity is all about love and acceptance when they see Christians promoting hate and bigotry. We can't tell them people of other faiths are bound for hell when they live and work and love alongside those very people. We can't tell them we know more than they do when they have the world of knowledge in their pockets.

Information is cheap in the Inventive Age. We are inundated with it all day, every day. Transferring information is simply not enough.

It is not that educated people are uninterested in information; the educated nature of Inventive Culture exists because of information. The shift is that people don't just want more information. We want meaningful information.

WE WANT INFORMATION THAT RESONATES.

Getting that information is surprisingly difficult. In the face of the massive amount of information in the world, people quickly get overwhelmed. That's why there are people who make a lot of money coming up with ways to help people sort through all the muck to find what's most interesting and relevant to them.

This is part of what makes social networking so attractive. Those systems operate under the assumption that people want the information those closest to them have. So rather than asking Google to scour the Internet and report the most linked-to websites, people look to their social networks to find out what their friends are reading and watching and discovering. They believe that if their friends like something or find it valuable, they will too. It's customizable information.

Evangelism in the Inventive Age calls for customized information. We can no longer assume we hold knowledge that other people don't have. We can no longer assume that if we just pass along a generic package of information it will do the job. No, if we are going to proclaim good news to people in the Inventive Age, we have to make the good news personal, meaningful, and relevant to the lives of the people we evangelize.

THE WEB OF AUTHORITY

The changes in education and our increasingly global mindset have altered the way people in the Inventive Age think about authority. For a person to click and drag an idea or a belief from being simply interesting to being life changing, they have to be convinced that this idea or belief is valid. In the previous ages, proving that validity was a simple matter of having a person in authority espouse that idea and pass it on to the masses. Now it's almost impossible to ascribe that level of authority to any one person or institution.

There are those who think people today have no respect for authority, that Inventive Age folks think they are smarter than everyone else and have little use for tradition or the wisdom of their elders. But I find the opposite to be the case. I find that Inventive Age people are eager to hear about ideas and beliefs. We love to hear the stories of other times and places and experience the traditions of the past. But we are far less inclined to blindly accept something as true just because someone told us to. In the Inventive Age people see themselves as the standard of authority.

How and why someone believes anything involve a complex mix of factors. So complex, in fact, that for a long time we have used metaphors to describe the way belief is formed. For a long time, the church has used an Industrial Age metaphor to explain how we come to believe what we believe. You've probably heard—or even used—the language of foundationalism, the idea that we have a handful of basic beliefs that serve as a foundation for all other belief. Foundationalism has given us the language

of anchors and slippery slopes and cornerstones and solid
rocks to describe faith.

It's not surprising that this metaphor took hold in
the latter part of the Industrial Age and gained strength
during the Information Age. One of the most amazing ar-
chitectural achievements of the twentieth century was the
skyscraper. This new building design was made possible
by the invention of the electric drill in the late nineteenth
century. The power of that drill allowed builders to anchor
a building in bedrock or create false bedrock on which the
frame of the building could rest.

So it goes with foundational belief systems—find
the stable, unchanging beliefs and build from there.

Foundationalism holds that beliefs are known and
justified based on their relationship to those basic beliefs.
The basic beliefs are thought to be self-evident. They don't
need to be justified by other beliefs. They stand firm all
by themselves. Think of the most famous line in the Declaration of Independence: "We hold these truths to be
self-evident, that all men are created equal, that they are
endowed by their Creator with certain unalienable Rights,
that among these are Life, Liberty and the pursuit of Hap-
piness." These ideals were considered so fundamental to
the shaping of the new nation that there was no need to
justify them.

Foundationalism found great favor with the early
twentieth century evangelists. As people from all over the
world started to pour into the growing cities of the United
States, Americans were bombarded with all sorts of new
religious ideas and had to make sophisticated distinctions
between faith claims. As the Industrial Age shifted into the
Information Age, churches found themselves eager to offer a kind of apologetic for their version of faith, generally
calculating that the more generic it was, the more people it
would attract. So the rambling story of faith was squeezed

into Four Spiritual Laws and Steps to Peace with God, meant to apply to all people in all situations. It was tracts and pamphlets and statements of faith, all meant to codify the faith in the simplest, most universal terms possible.

Over time, the distilled version of faith became foundational. It was like shorthand for what really matters. From an evangelistic standpoint, you needed only to convince others of those basic truths to bring about conversion. If you could get the targets of your evangelism to conform to this simple set of ideas, you had done your job.

But the Inventive Age requires a more particular faith to fit the more individualized sensibilities. We have far too much information available for us to accept simplistic formulas, far too much global exposure to settle for one-size-fits-all theology. We want our belief to match up with everything we know and experience and discover. That's why the Inventive Age calls for a way of understanding belief that makes room for new ideas without pushing out the old ones.

Instead of thinking of belief as a solid, unyielding building anchored in stone, we need to think of it as a dynamic process with a changing center and ever expanding and disintegrating edges.

BELIEF IS LESS LIKE A TOWER AND MORE LIKE A SPIDERWEB.

We tend to think of a spiderweb as fragile, but pound for pound, the silk of a spider's web is ten times stronger than steel. It can withstand extreme heat and extreme cold. It can be broken in several places and still hold a tremendous amount of weight relative to its size. It's a marvel of animal engineering.

Unlike a human-made building, the power of the web is not in what it is resting on, but in the connections of the strands. It can become detached from its original starting points and still hold together. It can even lose its center point and stay stable and strong.

The web of belief, an idea first proposed by the philosopher W. V. Quine in his book of the same name, suggests that our beliefs are interconnected, that instead of stacking up like building blocks, they spread out like strands of a web.

Beliefs held together in this web aren't dependent on a few bedrock truths. Instead, they connect in ever-changing ways. If one strand of belief is broken, others continue to hold the system together. New strands are woven in even as other strands disconnect and fall away.

People of the Inventive Age don't hand over authority easily. If we are going to accept a new idea, a new belief, it has to come from a source we trust. We determine our level of trust by considering what we already know to be true and aligning new ideas with those old beliefs. If that new thing fits, it will work its way into our web of belief. But if there is no connection, if this new thing feels false or ill fitting, it won't find a home in us. The challenge of evangelizing in the Inventive Age is to proclaim good news that connects to that web, that weaves its way into what's already there.

A POST-TRADITION PERSPECTIVE

The history of Christianity really should be called the history of Christianities. Since the first century, there have been hundreds of versions of our faith. So when someone talks about the Christian tradition, it's not always clear which of those hundreds of traditions they are referring to.

Christianity in the Inventive Age is no less diverse. According to the *World Christian Encyclopedia*, there were more than thirty-eight thousand registered denominations in the world in 2001.[6] There are more than a hundred Bible translations—and that's just in English.[7] Each of those translations tells the story in a particular way.

So when we engage someone in a conversation about Christianity, we ought to assume that person already has some kind of experience with Christianity, some opinions, and some well-thought-out ideas about faith. We can't assume they are starting with a blank slate. Even when we talk to people who have no experience with the Christian faith, we need to understand why that's the case—they may well have stayed away from Christianity on purpose.

Every conversation about Christianity is, to some degree, a cross-cultural engagement. We can't suggest that evangelism is meant to usher someone into that person's first-ever act of faith. For all we know, the person we're evangelizing has been living out some kind of faith for decades.

The increased globalization of the Inventive Age means we also can't assume their primary faith experiences will have been with Christianity. Even in my state of Minnesota, which is not really known for its ethnic diversity, I meet people who follow the Hindu faith, the Jewish faith, the Muslim faith, the Baha'i faith. I meet people who have left those faith traditions behind and have little interest in replacing them with something else. I meet people who have no faith background who are hungry for a spiritual story they can call their own. I meet people who are cobbling together fresh versions of faith that mix the best of their parents' Baptist faith with the hopeful ideas of their best friend's Buddhism, and are finding new roads to God.

Many people are spiritually engaged but have no allegiance to any particular form of religion. According to the 2008 American Religious Identification Survey, the fastest-growing group in the United States defines their religious affiliation as "None."[8] Others have no interest in religion of any variety, not even enough to call themselves atheists. They simply do not see themselves on the religious spectrum.

If we broaden our understanding of belief and worldview, we can no longer speak of "unbelievers." There are people who don't believe the way we do, but they are not "un" anything. They are something.

When I was a youth pastor, there was a big emphasis in the youth worker industry about the importance of reaching kids with the story of God by the time they were eighteen. There was talk of some major study that suggested that if a person didn't come to faith before the age of eighteen, they likely never would. The point was clear: reach kids while they're still in high school or risk losing them forever. That notion and statement fueled many youth ministry efforts.

I've been involved in formal ministry for more than twenty-five years, and I can tell you that it rarely matters *when* a person learns about the things of Jesus. We are all in need of hearing the story of God in new ways so it can have new power in our lives. Actually, I've found it's often more difficult to engage lifelong Christians in conversations about the wider scope of God's activity in the world than those who came to faith later in life.

The Inventive Age is a post-traditional age. There is no common faith we are asking others to join. Instead, there is a wide-ranging story that's big enough to include all comers.

PARTICULARITY OF PEOPLE

If there's one thing churches love to do, it's categorize people. Groups are based on marital status, age, gender, or the kind of work people do or the neighborhood they live in. Churches even hire separate staff people to work with these various groups—a children's pastor, a senior high pastor, a visitation pastor. It's as though the most important thing about each person is her demographic information.

But in every other part of our lives we are expected to see ourselves as far more than our demographic categories. In the Inventive Age, we are expected to know ourselves, and know ourselves well.

There is no end to the resources that help us learn more about ourselves: psychological categories, personality types, body types, blood types. We can distinguish ourselves as sanguine or choleric, introvert or extrovert, idealist or artisan, ENFP or ISTJ.

In the Inventive Age, we aren't interested in knowing ourselves just for the fun of it. We truly believe that the things that make us unique really matter. We want to understand what makes us happy, what drives us, what hurts us, what inspires us. We want to understand all of this because we believe every human being has something to offer the world. And the more we know about ourselves, the better equipped we are to give what we have.

Our belief in the uniqueness of each person means we have little patience for generic anything. We want our food to be local, seasonal, and organic instead of cheap and processed. We are drawn to authentic expressions of belief, whether that belief is in the superiority of the small family farm or in the goodness of the gospel message. Anything that feels premade, prepackaged, or premeditated rings hollow.

I play basketball with an eclectic group of guys at a health club. One of the guys, Daniel, is fairly new to the area. Not long ago, he pulled me aside and said, "What do you know about Life Church?"

"Quite a bit," I said. "Tim over there is the pastor."

"Oh no."

I looked at Daniel and waited for him to elaborate. He hesitated, then said, "I don't want to embarrass him, but could you explain something to me? The other day my doorbell rang, and when I looked out I saw a van with the church logo on it. There was no way I was going to open the door and get stuck talking to some religious guy who came to my house. When they were gone, I opened the door to see if they'd left a pamphlet or something. I find this huge bucket full of stuff for the house. It was wrapped and even had a bow on it. I don't want this thing. But now I feel like I'm supposed to do something, like I'm obligated to them. I don't get it. What do they want from me?"

I asked Daniel to send me a picture of the bucket. It really was something to behold. It was a large blue bucket with a handwritten note taped to the side. I can see a bunch of hangers, a tape measure, a package of pens, lightbulbs, hand soap, a flashlight, and all kinds of other supplies a person might need after moving into a new house. It was all encased in plastic wrap and topped off with a bow.

A few days later I asked Tim, the pastor, about the bucket. He explained that there are about a hundred move-ins each month in the affluent suburb surrounding the church. The church wanted to change the relationship people have with churches, so they came up with the buckets as a way to welcome folks to the neighborhood. From Tim's perspective, it was a way of telling people that the church was a good neighbor, eager to help in any way it could. "Most churches want something from people," he told me. "We wanted to change that and start by giving something."

Tim shared stories of many people who expressed their appreciation for the bucket. They understood that the church was being thoughtful.

But not Daniel. He felt obligated by the bucket. Those strangers had given him a gift, and now he felt he should do something in return. As an intentional non-churchgoer, Daniel didn't want a gift from a church. He was taken aback to know that people at this church had his address, knew he was new to town, and had walked up the driveway to his door. Daniel would never darken the doorstep of a church, and he certainly didn't want them darkening his.

Daniel told me he'd given the bucket to a homeless shelter, a process that involved him figuring out where he could find a homeless shelter, driving to it, and explaining that he didn't want a receipt for tax purposes. Instead of a welcome gift, the bucket became a source of obligation and inconvenience.

I know the people of Life Church only had good intentions. But they also had a generic plan. In the Inventive Age, generic outreach plans, presentations, and evangelism are riddled with risk.

The desire to know ourselves and be known by others might sound egotistical. But this sense of particularity is actually deeply communal. The impulse to understand what makes us unique gives us a sense of purpose and invitation. The more we know about ourselves, the more we recognize what it is we have to give to the world, what it is we can contribute. And it inspires us to seek out others, recognize what is unique in them, and work collectively to create the future.

This is the way of Jesus.

Jesus practiced a first-name faith, a particular faith that was directed specifically at whomever he was talking to at the moment. The Jesus we find in the Gospels never gives the same answer twice.

Jesus spoke with all kinds of people who wanted to know how to enter the kingdom of God. And every one of them got a different, uniquely personal response. For Nicodemus, the answer was to be born again. The rich young ruler was told to sell all he had. The woman at the well was sent to tell others, while the healed leper was instructed not to tell anyone and instead go to the temple priests and show them what Jesus had done. Mary was to have peace; the woman caught in adultery was to leave her current life. Peter was asked to die with Jesus, and Judas was told to do what he planned to do.

Those are just the stories we know. John reminds us there are plenty more.[9]

As they followed in the way of Jesus, early Christians were radically committed to forging a faith that fit the people. The theological debate of the first century was centered on whether non-Jews—the Gentiles—needed to convert and become culturally Jewish in order to be part of the work God was doing through Jesus. The book of Acts—which I will in a bit suggest as a model for evangelism—tells us that the answer was a resounding "No!" This sensibility of inclusion and invitation has been part of the Christian faith ever since.

Evangelism in the Inventive Age requires us to follow the same path of the early church by proclaiming good news that is particular, not generic.

THE STORY OF GOD IS PLAYING OUT IN EACH ONE OF US.

Evangelism isn't about adding something new to the lives of others. It's about drawing out what God is already doing in them. Like good midwives, we are called to facilitate the birth of renewed hope, renewed purpose, renewed connection in those we evangelize. We are, in the words of Jesus, helping them to be born again.

It takes effort to make evangelism personal. It takes commitment to know and understand people as individuals. It takes time to offer more than a four-point argument or a premade set of beliefs. Proclaiming the good news in the Inventive Age will demand new ideas and beliefs and skills. And it will be worth it.

SECTION 4

GOOD NEWS THAT CONNECTS

The central narrative of the Christian story has always been one of connection and embrace. From the very beginning, our story has been about God's far-reaching embrace of the entire cosmos, the whole of creation. And yet it is also about God's intimate connection to humanity. God is as big as the universe and as close as our breath. That's the story we've told from the first verses of Genesis to the last words of Revelation. It's the story we continue to tell.

Evangelism involves connecting people to this story in ways that ring true, that resonate. Evangelism happens when the Spirit of God that's alive in each person finds its point of connection with the larger story of God. The apostle Paul writes, "The same Spirit agrees with our spirit, that we are God's children."[10] When we understand evangelism as this kind of spiritual resonance, we can't be content with a generic package that we label "Good News."

As Christians, we believe that each of us is created in the image of God, that we bear the mark of God. Genesis 1:27 tells us: "God created humanity in God's own image, in the divine image God created them, male and female God created them."

Each of us bears the image of God.

For centuries, theologians have wondered what part of humanity reflects this image. Some suggest it's intellect, our ability to reason. Some suggest it's the everlasting soul. Some say it's our innate sense of morality. Some see humanity as having been created in the community of God—an idea they get from the preceding passage, in which God says, "Let *us* make. . ." Others believe we find the image of God reflected in our capacity to love. Still others suggest the emphasis is on our ability to create and be co-creators with God.

I think it's all of these—and a few more. I believe we also find the image of God in our passions, our hopes and dreams. And I believe we find the image of God in our temperament, in the way each of us sees and interacts with the world.

Consider Paul's imagery in the letters to the Romans and the Corinthians. He writes of Christians being one body made of many parts. The image of God in each one of us creates the body of Christ.[11]

THE PASSIONS IN US REFLECT THE PASSIONS OF GOD.

When our evangelistic efforts help connect a person's passions and gifts and temperaments to those same aspects of God, then we have certainly proclaimed good news.

WHO WE ARE

To do that, of course, we need to figure out what people are passionate about, what drives them and scares them and inspires them. I believe these passions and fears are the framework around which we build our understanding of God, humanity, and the story in which we all exist. If we want to invite people to join the Spirit of God alive in them with what God is doing in the world, we need to know what that Spirit is up to in each person.

While there are all kinds of ways to think about and categorize the human temperament, I've been greatly influenced by the Enneagram. It's a personality assessment

tool that suggests there are nine categories for understanding our temperament and perspective. It's not the
answer to all human situations or struggles, nor is it a
summary of all that God can do in the lives of human
beings. But I've found it to be an essential lens through
which to understand myself, others, and God. You might
have your own paradigm through which you understand
the ways the Spirit of God lives in humanity. This descrip-
tion is not meant to compete with that, but perhaps can
add to it and encourage you to lean into your understanding as a means of helping the story of God connect with
others.

When it comes to evangelism, I find that one of the
most helpful aspects of the Enneagram is the suggestion
that each person has a complex set of passions—what
they want in life—and fears—what they seek to prevent.
The Enneagram is a sophisticated and complex system,
so for the purposes of this book I've come up with my
own summary of the passions and fears associated
with each of the nine types. I'll include some thoughts
of the two leading voices of the Enneagram, Don Riso
and Russ Hudson, and a few other leading authors and
practitioners of the Enneagram. You can find out far
more—and even figure out your Enneagram type—at
www.enneagraminstitute.com.

We'll start by looking at the passion part of this understanding of human beings. *Passion* is a word that gets
thrown around a lot. People use it to describe anything
that excites them. But when I talk about passion, I'm talking about more than the things that make us happy or fill
us with joy. I'm talking about our deepest desires for who
we could be and what we want from life. These are the
subconscious desires that inhabit us as much as we hold
them. We don't choose these orientations. They are "built
in." Because we are particular people, understanding a
person's passion is central to evangelism in the Inventive
Age.

PASSION

The Enneagram suggests nine life passions, and I find all of them important and essential to God's work in the world. Each of us finds resonance with one or maybe two or three, but all of us will have one that is primary. The idea is that God embodies all of these passions and that each of us connects with God through the passions we share with God.

Our primary passion orients our internal narrative. Each of us has a deep desire to be something, to be a certain kind of person who brings about particular goodness in the world. Even when we're not aware of it, this longing shapes our interactions, our work, our view of humanity, and our understanding of God. When we see the story of God through our internal narrative, we find ourselves integrated with God.

Here are the nine passions and each type's deepest longings:

1. **Be Good:** To have integrity, to be above reproach, to be right, and to overcome moral adversity and make the world better.

2. **Be Loved:** To express my feelings for others, to be needed and appreciated, to experience love, closeness, sharing, family, and friendship.

3. **Be Valuable:** To develop my passions and contribute my abilities to the world. To motivate others to greater personal achievements than they thought they were capable of.

4. **Be Themselves:** To know that I am uniquely talented and possess special, one-of-a-kind gifts. To protect my emotions and sense of myself.

5. **Be Capable:** To find out why things are the way they are through my own intelligence and effort. By understanding the world, I can make it better for myself and others.

6. **Be Secure:** To live beyond my fears and insecurity and find security, support, and consistency in my relationships.

7. **Be Fulfilled:** To be free to experience life fully and embrace everything that brings me joy.

8. **Be in Control:** To be my own person, to be strong and self-sufficient. To have my ideas heard and thought of as important and innovative.

9. **Be Balanced:** To have inner stability and peace of mind in my relationships, to diminish conflict and bring unity.[12]

These passions aren't limited to what a person wants from life. They also frame the way people engage with others. The Be Loved people, for example, tend to be nurturing and caring, and even possessive in their relationships. The Be Capable people are very perceptive and great at reading people, but they keep their observations and feelings to themselves. The Be in Control folks give off an air of self-confidence, while the Be Valuable people easily adapt to meet the needs of others.

All of this means that a person who approaches life and relationships with confidence is living out a very different core passion than a person who knows how to adapt herself to fit the situation or relationship. And these different core passions mean that each of these people will resonate with a different piece of the story of God.

Now here's where this stuff gets really interesting for me. When I was learning about God as a new Christian, there were a handful of ways people talked about God. There was Lord, Creator, the Almighty, Father, and a few others that, for me at least, all pointed to just a few aspects of who God is. But as I studied the Bible and learned more about the ancient story of our faith, I learned that the Hebrew language describes God in ways that bring all kinds of richness to the character and activity of God.

What I find intriguing about the Hebrew names for God is that most of them describe God's relationship with humanity. They are intimate, active images of a God who lives and works through God's people. I don't think it's a coincidence that many of the Hebrew names for God resonate with the passions embedded in each of us.

As you read through the chart on page 53, you likely resonate strongly with at least one of those passions and maybe a couple of others. There is a driving force in you, a passion for framing your life in a certain way. And that is the way you connect with God.

Of course you might connect with God in lots of ways, but when you are truly aware of your passion, you know that when you are living out that inner calling, that's when you feel like you are in the God groove. My friend Thom calls it firing on all cylinders. You know when it's happening because everything about what you're doing or thinking or discovering just fits.

We also tend to believe that our way is the best way, that our passion is the truest image of God. But God is not somehow contained in only one or two of these passions. God is in all of them. And it takes all of them for us to know the fullness of God's image.

Think of a photo mosaic. Viewed as a whole, it appears to be one image when in fact it's made up of hun-

BE	GOD	HEBREW NAME
BE GOOD	GOD HEALS	JEHOVAH-ROPHE
BE LOVED	GOD IS LOVE	EL SHADDAI
BE VALUABLE	GOD IS MOST HIGH	EL ELYON
BE THEMSELVES	GOD CALLS	YAHWEH NISSI
BE CAPABLE	GOD SEES	EL ROI
BE SECURE	GOD PROVIDES	YAHWEH JIREH
BE FULFILLED	GOD IS EVERLASTING	EL OLAM
BE IN CONTROL	GOD FREES	YAHWEH SHALOM
BE BALANCED	GOD IS ONE	EHYEH-ASHER-EHYEH

dreds, even thousands of smaller images. Each one of the nine passions is an essential part of helping humanity thrive. But together they show us the image of God.

When we invite people to see that what is most vital in them is a reflection of God, they start to see that their story and God's story are one and the same. They begin to see that they are an indispensable part of the whole.

FEAR

On our best days, it's our passions that drive us. But each of the nine types also has a deep fear—that secret place of insecurity and pain we hope never shows. If the good news of God is going to resonate with us fully, it can't just be about connecting with our desires. It must embrace our fears as well.

The fears for each of the types can be articulated like this:

1. Be Good: I'm flawed.

2. Be Loved: I will be rejected.

3. Be Valuable: I'm worthless.

4. Be Themselves: I'm ordinary.

5. Be Capable: I'm of no use.

6. Be Secure: I'm alone.

7. Be Fulfilled: I'm stuck.

8. Be in Control: I will be harmed.

9. Be Balanced: I will be conflicted.

We tend to think of fear as a negative thing, something that no good Christian should experience. But these
core fears are different. They are the kind of fear that lives
deep in our souls, the kind that longs for life to look different than it does.

As I've become more familiar with the nine types, I
see them playing out everywhere, even in the Bible. I was
especially struck by the parallels between the nine fears
and the Sermon on the Mount. Obviously, Jesus wasn't
talking about the Enneagram as he preached to the crowd.
But he was talking about their deepest fears. These particular messages rang true for some of his listeners in ways
they didn't with others. When you look at the list, you
might find yourself connecting with some of the promises
differently than others.

In the sermon, Jesus tells people that God is on the
side of the helpless, the grieving, the humble, those longing for righteousness. God is on the side of the merciful,
the pure, the harassed, the insulted. Jesus tells his listeners that God knows their fears and will meet them in those
dark places with the promise of hope. In Matthew 5:3-12
Jesus says:

> Blessed are the poor in spirit, for theirs is the
> kingdom of heaven.
>
> Blessed are those who mourn, for they will be
> comforted.
>
> Blessed are the meek, for they will inherit the
> earth.
>
> Blessed are those who hunger and thirst for righ-
> teousness, for they will be filled.
>
> Blessed are the merciful, for they will be shown
> mercy.

Blessed are the pure in heart, for they will see God.

Blessed are the peacemakers, for they will be called children of God.

Blessed are those who are persecuted because of righteousness, for theirs is the kingdom of heaven.

Blessed are you when people insult you, persecute you and falsely say all kinds of evil against you because of me. Rejoice and be glad, because great is your reward in heaven, for in the same way they persecuted the prophets who were before you.[13]

These dark places are not problematic in and of themselves. Like our passions, they can be places of intimate connection with God. But too often we live out our fears far more than we live out our passions. A person whose passion is to be loved can be a caring, giving, helpful friend. But if that person lives out of her fear of being rejected, she can become manipulative, controlling, and jealous. When we connect the stories of others to the story of God, we need to help them see that, while God can heal and offer hope in the midst of their fears, it is their passions that will bring them more fully into the story.

WE DON'T CHOOSE THESE PASSIONS OR FEARS.

They live with us like a beckoning friend and a dark passenger. The passions call us to a full life, while the fears can cause us to destroy what is most important to us. They

BE	FEAR	SERMON
BE GOOD	I'M FLAWED	BLESSED ARE THOSE WHO HUNGER AND THIRST FOR RIGHTEOUSNESS
BE LOVED	I WILL BE REJECTED	BLESSED ARE THE MERCIFUL
BE VALUABLE	I'M WORTHLESS	BLESSED ARE THE PURE IN HEART
BE THEMSELVES	I'M ORDINARY	BLESSED ARE THOSE WHO MOURN
BE CAPABLE	I'M OF NO USE	BLESSED ARE THOSE WHO ARE PERSECUTED BECAUSE OF RIGHTEOUSNESS
BE SECURE	I'M ALONE	BLESSED ARE THE POOR IN SPIRIT
BE FULFILLED	I'M STUCK	BLESSED ARE THE MERCIFUL
BE IN CONTROL	I'LL BE HARMED	BLESSED ARE YOU WHEN PEOPLE INSULT YOU, PERSECUTE YOU AND FALSELY SAY ALL KINDS OF EVIL AGAINST YOU
BE BALANCED	I'LL BE CONFLICTED	BLESSED ARE THE PEACEMAKERS

are simply with us, and we often must identify them in order to see beyond them.

My wife, Shelley, told me a story about an eighty-six-year-old man who had been married for more than forty years. This man valued loyalty above all else. He was passionate about his connections with people and ideas. Shelley explained that every day when he woke up, his first thought was, "Today is the day when my wife will leave me." His deepest fear was that he would be abandoned by someone he loved. But he knew this was fear talking, so rather than let the fear rule him, he would turn to his wife and remind himself that he could trust her.

THE DRIVING EMOTION

In terms of evangelism, it can be a bit overwhelming to find a way to understand each of the nine types well enough to proclaim good news in such a way that it will resonate with the individual passions and fears of everyone we meet. But the types don't stand in isolation from one another. They have all kinds of overlap, ways in which people of different types will have similar responses to problems or challenges or pain.

Hudson and Riso arranged the types in three different clusters of emotional response and resonance: shame, anxiety, and anger.[14]

SHAME	ANXIETY	ANGER
BE LOVED, BE VALUABLE, BE THEMSELVES	BE CAPABLE, BE SECURE, BE FULFILLED	BE GOOD, BE IN CONTROL, BE BALANCED

People in these type clusters will connect with a story in similar ways. For example, the Bible's opening narrative, the creation story, holds different points of connection for these different clusters.

The Be Loved, Be Valuable, Be Themselves people understand shame. They don't need anyone to point out the ways they have failed or fallen—they know it like they know their names. So when these folks hear the story of Adam and Eve eating the forbidden fruit and being reprimanded by God, they feel it deeply:

> During that day's cool evening breeze, they heard the sound of the LORD God walking in the garden; and the man and his wife hid themselves from the LORD God in the middle of the garden's trees. The LORD God called to the man and said to him, "Where are you?" The man replied, "I heard your sound in the garden; I was afraid because I was naked, and I hid myself."[15]

Those in the shame cluster connect to this story on a gut level—they know what self-doubt feels like. They tap into the feeling of being naked and ashamed. They know what it's like to have failed someone, to disappoint and lose face.

Those who wrestle with anxiety might not think twice about this part of the story. But they find familiarity in the earlier part of the story:

> The snake was the most intelligent of all the wild animals that the LORD God had made. He said to the woman, "Did God really say that you shouldn't eat from any tree in the garden?" The woman said to the snake, "We may eat the fruit of the garden's trees but not the fruit of the tree in the middle of the garden. God said, 'Don't eat from it, and don't touch it, or you will die.'" The snake said to the woman, "You won't die! God knows that on the day you eat from it, you will

see clearly and you will be like God, knowing good and evil."[16]

This part of the story resonates for people whose core fear is being without guidance. The uncertainty beneath the serpent's questioning pushes at this cluster's anxiety about what and whom they can trust. This part of the story feels painfully familiar to those in the anxiety cluster.

The anxiety of these types leads them to work and rework conversations, to doubt what was said, to fear that they don't know the truth. They will talk themselves into and out of commitments and ideas as they try to get rid of their pervasive worry. They are filled with anxiety in ways the other types could never imagine.

The Be Good, Be in Control, and Be Balanced types certainly understand self-doubt and self-loathing, but they are far more familiar with anger. They are fiery people and know what it's like to fight against their own rage. So they understand stories of people having to keep their passions in check, like the story of Cain and Abel:

> Some time later, Cain presented an offering to the Lord from the land's crops while Abel presented his flock's oldest offspring with their fat. The Lord looked favorably on Abel and his sacrifice but didn't look favorably on Cain and his sacrifice. Cain became very angry and looked resentful. The Lord said to Cain, "Why are you angry, and why do you look so resentful? If you do the right thing, won't you be accepted? But if you don't do the right thing, sin will be waiting at the door ready to strike! It will entice you, but you must rule over it." Cain said to his brother Abel, "Let's go out to the field." When they were in the field, Cain attacked his brother Abel and killed him.[17]

Those in the anger cluster hear that story and can feel the rage of Cain rising in them. They feel for Cain and share his sense of indignation. Cain isn't the villain in this story; he is a man to be pitied, for his rage got the best of him. Those who know the power of their own anger find themselves empathizing with Cain in ways the other types won't.

One story, filled with so much richness, so much emotion.

One story made better by particular connections to particular people.

Central to any evangelistic effort is that people find themselves in the reality of God's story. And as the story of God plays out in the Bible, it's clear that it is a story of anger, shame, and worry.

STRUGGLE

Another lens through which to see the types is the response in *struggle*. One cluster is compliant and engaging, one is confident and assertive, and one retreats and is withdrawn. Some scholars see these three responses as human versions of the classic animal responses to a threat: submission, fight, or flight.[18] The gospel will resonate differently for each of these personality clusters.

COMPLIANT	CONFIDENT	WITHDRAWN
BE GOOD, BE LOVED, BE SECURE	BE VALUABLE, BE FULFILLED, BE IN CONTROL	BE THEMSELVES, BE CAPABLE, BE BALANCED

Those in the compliant cluster get really nervous about the possibility of being rejected or abandoned. Faced with a situation that feels chaotic or haphazard, they seek out rules and patterns, anything to help them make sense of what's going on. In times of crisis or opposition, they get mired in ambiguity and uncertainty. Instead of following their own sense of purpose, they will defer to others—even when they don't agree with them.

People in the confident cluster don't like to be uncomfortable. So when they find themselves in a situation they don't like or when they are feeling an emotion they would rather not feel, they puff up and become full of themselves. They will stop listening to others they see as a source of their discomfort and rely on their own understanding and ideas.

The types prone to withdrawal will move away from challenging situations as quickly as possible. If physical distance isn't an option, they will remove themselves emotionally. When they do, they start to lose sight of what is really going on and start telling themselves that their perception of a situation is reality, even if that perception is skewed by fear or anxiety.

These differing responses play into evangelism in really interesting ways. If we suggest to a person prone to withdrawal that they need to connect with God through private prayer and study, they'll be all over that. It suits the way they find comfort in difficult situations. But for the confident types, nothing is less appealing that being alone with their thoughts. They want action. They don't want to waste time considering ideas; they want to do something about those ideas.

Even the way we organize our churches can trigger these responses in people. Churches steeped in the practices of liturgical prayer and ritual are incredibly appealing to compliant types who find great comfort in patterns and order and clear expectations. A free-form worship style where people dance in the aisle or speak up from their seats during prayer might feel just right to the confident types who want to know they have a voice in the community.

The various traditions of the Christian church have their own personalities as well. And while I won't push this connection so far as to suggest that there are Enneagram Type 1 churches and Enneagram Type 8 churches, I do find that certain traditions fit certain types better than others.

For example, some traditions are centered on the idea that people are depraved, broken, and in need of change. Within these traditions, there is a heavy emphasis on people doing something that will heal that brokenness. It might be assenting to a certain set of beliefs, taking the Eucharist, being baptized, or practicing confession. The mode is not as important as the notion that something is broken and needs fixing. In those traditions, the good news of the gospel is that Jesus heals and restores and repairs.

Those traditions hold great appeal for Be Good types. They go right to the heart of the fears of inadequacy and brokenness this type wrestles with. And, more importantly, they provide a release from those fears. The good news of restoration resonates.

Other traditions are based on the idea that God promises abundant life. In these traditions, the gospel isn't about solving a problem or fixing something that's broken. It's about the fulfillment of a promise. That's their good news. The Be Fulfilled types are drawn to these traditions, where they can connect their longings to the story of God's promises.

Some traditions make it clear you are loved. The gospel call will start with God's love for you and will find a way to finish there as well. For the Be Loved type, it's not possible to hear that message too often. On the other hand, my friend Brad said to me, "If I go to one more church where we spend half an hour singing about how much God loves us and not a word about how we should bring about changes in the abusive structures in our world, I might never go back to any church."

Brad is a Be in Control type. His passion is to be free, so he will work as hard as he needs to in order to free himself and others from systems that entrap them. For Brad, hearing that God loves him is a starting place, but that love needs to lead to freedom.

Pam was raised in a tradition that stressed how unique she is. She knew she was knit together by God in her mother's womb and that God had counted all the hairs on her head. She knew she was as unique as a snowflake and had a purpose in life that was hers and hers alone. But Pam isn't motivated by thinking that she's unique. She wants to be useful. She wants to be part of something big and meaningful, not the most special person on a list of one.

Each tradition emphasizes parts of the human story of life with God. And that's how it should be—if we were all telling the same story, we'd leave out whole swaths of the population. At the same time, when a person only knows one part of the story—a part that doesn't resonate for her—she begins to wonder if this faith is the right fit for her.

That doesn't mean we have to change our traditions or radically alter how we tell the story. Instead, we need to open ourselves and our communities to the larger story being played out in the lives of other people. Instead of asking others to conform to our version of the story, we can allow them to show us where they find those places of resonance. When they do, well, that's when the beautiful mosaic picture of the image of God comes into view.

Of course there is far more to people than these personality orientations. We're all able to see the world from perspectives other than our own. But as evangelists, it's crucial that we move beyond communicating pre-packaged information for all people and recognize that we are relating to real people with real passions and fears and preferences. We are connecting people to a rich story that finds a home in each person in a unique way.

SEEING BUT NOT PERCEIVING

Perhaps the biggest hurdle to evangelism in the Inventive Age is our own perception. The lenses through which each of us sees the world can be so powerful that they distort our view. We can start to live with a kind of tunnel vision where we only see what's right in front of us, missing the good things that lie on the periphery.

We tend to think that the story that resonates with us ought to be the story that resonates with others. I am drawn to the freedom and acceptance I find in God. But if I frame the good news as freedom to those who long for security and structure, I've lost them. For them, freedom is anything but good news—it is the problem.

Even when we know this is true, it's incredibly difficult to move beyond our perceptions and truly see people for who they are.

In their book *The Invisible Gorilla: How Our Intuitions Deceive Us*,[19] Christopher Chabris and Daniel Simons explore how it is possible for us to miss seeing things, even when they are right in front of us.

Their premier experiment involves showing people a short video clip of six people passing two basketballs around the group. Three of the people are wearing white shirts and three are wearing black. Viewers are asked to silently count how many times the people in white shirts pass the ball to one another. The clip lasts about a minute and a half.

Now in the midst of the balls being passed around, a full-sized person in a black gorilla suit walks from the right side of the screen and stands in the middle of the group. The gorilla faces the camera, points at himself with his thumbs, and does a little dance before exiting on the left side of the screen. The gorilla is on the screen for nine seconds.

At the end of the video, the audience is asked if they saw the gorilla. Usually, less than half the audience will say yes.

I use this video when I speak to groups, and I've done this experiment more than one hundred times. Every time, there are people who completely miss the gorilla.

Then I show the video again. This time, everyone sees the gorilla, and the room fills with laughter and disbelief as people wonder how they missed something so obvious the first time around.

I talked with the authors of *The Invisible Gorilla* to find out more about their experiments in perception. Chabris and Simons told me that the reason people don't see the gorilla is not that they aren't paying attention. They actually see the gorilla with their eyes—the people in white are walking around it and avoiding it as they pass the ball. But in their attempt to pay attention to the people in white, they ignored the people in black, including the gorilla. So while their eyes registered the presence of the

gorilla, their brains determined that it wasn't relevant to
the task at hand and let the information go.

Interestingly, I find that the people who miss seeing
the gorilla usually get the correct number of passes between the people in the white shirts. They were paying
attention to what they were told was important and fulfilled the duty assigned to them.

Chabris and Simons have done many experiments
that demonstrate what they also call the "Illusion of
Attention." They explained to me that this is not an
occasional act but rather the way most of us function all
the time. I guess that's a good thing. There are far too
many stimuli around us for us to pay attention to all of
them. We can't notice every bird or sound or heartbeat or
idea—our brains would get overwhelmed. So we organize
our lives by a subconscious set of priorities.

Chabris and Simons call this our "attention set."[20]
It's what you know to pay attention to. For example, they
write about a study of sixty-two accidents in which a car
struck a motorcycle. The accidents had something interesting in common: none of the car drivers had a motorcycle
license. Their conclusion? What helps people see motorcycles is not those "Start Seeing Motorcycles" bumper stick-
ers but having personal experience riding motorcycles.[21]

The authors explained that these attention experiments reveal two things: that we are missing a lot of what
goes on around us and that we have no idea how much
we are missing.

WE THINK WE PAY ATTENTION TO FAR MORE THAN WE ACTUALLY DO.

There's little we can do about that fact except re-mind ourselves that we have false confidence in our pow-ers of perception.

This is what happens when we are engaged with the story of God. Our own root story, our passions and fears, create our attention set. Like the people who were busy counting passes, we all miss much of what is going on in the lives of the people around us. But for us to evangelize in the Inventive Age, we need to remind ourselves again that we have false confidence in our powers of perception. There will always be more to the story than what we know and see. That's why we need others to join in with the story and show us what we're missing.

PAYING ATTENTION

Before we can proclaim good news to anyone, we have to start paying attention to what kind of news they need. That means finding ways to expand our attention set and make room for the ways God's story has been playing out in the lives of others right before our eyes.

There are lots of ways to do this, but I'd like to focus on three that I have found to be particularly helpful in my efforts to be open to other ways of understanding God's story: listening, going first, and non-identical repetition.

Listening

Evangelism in the Inventive Age will require listen-ing not only to someone's words but also to the story they are living.

There is indeed an art to listening well. I know this because it's taken me a long time to learn it. Listening can be especially hard for those of us trained as pastors or preachers. In my four years of seminary, I took no fewer than four courses on preaching, but active listening was relegated to one class session in a Christian education course. I was trained to be a talker.

Being a listener requires a different skill set. It means starting not with answers but with questions. If I want to know someone, if I want to discover the story they are living, then I need to ask about it and really listen to what they say. Some of us don't know how to do this. We don't know how to move beyond the basic "Hi, how are you?" conversation starters.

But I'm always surprised by how eager people are to move past the niceties and talk about what matters to them, what they want out of life, what they worry about. In other words, their passions and fears. When we show genuine interest and curiosity toward the people we talk to—whether they are people we've known for years or total strangers—we start to see that those passions and fears live pretty close to the surface.

My friend David is a former youth worker. He told me about riding on a bus for some youth group trip. One of the kids, a fifteen-year-old boy, was having a tough time connecting with others and with God. This boy sat on the bus listening to music. David sat down beside him and asked what he was listening to. The boy took out one of his earbuds and gave it to David so they could listen together. Each time the song changed, David would ask, "What is it about this song you like?" As David listened to the boy's responses, he began to notice that all of the songs were about losing someone you love. By paying attention and listening to the boy's story, David could see that love, security, and consistency were going to be his connecting points.

We might not all have such a clear inroad to another person's passions and fears, but by listening for the themes that keep coming up—loneliness or loss, dreams and plans, the search for purpose and meaning—we can start to find ways to proclaim particular good news.

Going first

Listening doesn't mean you should never talk. One of the most meaningful ways to tap into someone's passions and fears is to talk about your own.

Many of us seem to have no idea that it's okay to talk about these things, especially in the context of faith. When we talk about how we connect with God's story through our own passions and fears, we give other people permission to do the same. For many people, it will be like a light coming on.

I was at a men's breakfast with a group of guys from our church, and we were talking about our own personalities and ways of seeing the world. I talked about my recurring nightmares. One involves me being chased in a park and getting trapped in a public restroom by people who want to hurt me. The other is a dream in which the wall behind the headboard of my bed is on fire and starting to collapse. This dream started when our daughter was a baby and often slept with us in our bed. This dream was so vivid that I would often jump out of bed, put my hands on the wall, and yell at my wife to get the baby out of the room.

Even though this is a group of men I know and trust, it was embarrassing to tell them about these dreams—they reveal fears and weakness in me that I'd rather keep to myself. But by talking about these dreams, I let others know it was okay to talk about their nightmares. Theirs were just as revealing:

- I am invisible. I try and try and try to get some- one's attention, but no one sees me.

- I am trying to save my family from danger (often spiders), but they don't listen to me. They won't move away from the danger.

- I drive off a bridge and fall into nothingness.

- I'm about to teach a class and I'm not prepared.

- I'm being chased and can't outrun the person.

- I have tornado dreams whenever I feel like my life is out of control. The people and places change, but there are always tornadoes.

Talking about the things that haunt us at night was a great way to understand one another. But someone had to go first. Someone had to open the door to that conver- sation so others would know it was okay to be vulnerable.

Non-identical repetition

The notion of non-identical repetition is that some stories in our lives repeat over time. It's something I no- ticed a few years ago when we were reading through Genesis at our church. We noticed that some stories in the Bible come back around again—not in the sense of Jesus quoting the Old Testament or the separate birth narra- tives in Luke and Matthew. I mean stories of one group of people excluding another, only to find out that those are the people favored by God. Stories of fathers and sons struggling to hold on to power or carry on a legacy. Sto- ries of forgotten people becoming the main characters in the story. This non-identical repetition reminds us that the story of God is rich and complex and keeps cycling around to show us what's important.

Not long ago I was talking with my friend Joseph, who is also "my" rabbi. We were talking about some difficult things I had been experiencing recently, and he said, "I will be praying with you as you walk through these waters."

I knew what he was referring to—the people of Israel passing through the parted waters of the Red Sea as they left captivity in Egypt and headed toward the promised land.

With this simple statement, Joseph put my story into a larger context. He reminded me that I am not alone. For me, a Be in Control person who fears being trapped, the good news in that moment was for him to tell me that my circumstances don't have to win. He proclaimed the news that God is walking with me and leading me.

Showing people their stories through the lens of the larger story of God is an essential part of evangelism in the Inventive Age. For this to happen, we, both individually and as communities, need to know that story well. The Bible, then, can't just be a record of the past. It has to be a living set of stories that give us new ways to know ourselves and connect with God.

Each of these ways of paying attention to others can quickly fall into the category of a sales pitch. But if our desire to know where God is at work in others is genuine, if we are truly looking to connect people to God in meaningful ways, then listening to them, being vulnerable with them, showing them that their stories are part of something bigger, are not methods or tactics. They are relationship skills that lead us not only to more effective evangelism but also to more effective humanity.

SECTION 5

THE ACTS OF EVANGELISM

At Solomon's Porch, our sermons are a bit unusual. Instead of centering the sermon on a specific topic or following a predetermined order that prescribes certain readings for each Sunday of the liturgical year, we read entire books of the Bible out loud. We take one book at a time and read a chapter or two a week until we finish it. We read what the Bible has to say to us and talk about how we are implicated by what we're reading. It's been a tremendous learning experience for all of us to let the Bible speak for itself, instead of having an "expert" give a sermon based on a few snippets.

A couple of years ago, we spent about nine months reading Acts. It's one of the books of the Bible named for its subject, not its author. During the course of those nine months, it was clear to us that this book is more than just the story of the early church. It is an epic tale of the development of our faith. While the book has also been called the Acts of the Apostles, the cast of characters extends far beyond the handful of men we tend to think of as the apostles. There are Jews and Gentiles, men and women, community leaders and up-and-comers. We find out how Saul became Paul, how Peter realized that the faith was more open than he had thought, and how the faith of a few Jews in Jerusalem spread to the rest of the known world to include Gentiles as well as Jews.

This expansive, epic story is a unique record of the earliest evangelistic efforts of Jesus' followers. Those of us seeking to evangelize in the Inventive Age could do worse than to take our cues from the book of Acts.

The very name of the book gives us some ideas about how we ought to approach evangelism. The word *acts* can mean lots of things. It can be short for *actions*. The book of Acts is a collection of stories about what those first Christians were doing. It reads like a fast-paced movie that cuts from action sequence to action sequence while the players sort out how this new faith will work.

Acts can also be short for the *activities* of the early church. The word *activities* has a broader connotation than the word *actions*. It's the framework in which the actions happen and the characteristics of those actions. So while an action might be teaching or preaching or arguing, the related activity might be training or educating or planning.

Acts can also be thought of as the sections of a play. Certainly, the book of Acts has the feel of being the first act of a longer story. It's the book that launches us into the history of the church, the story we see playing out in the remaining books of the New Testament.

For the rest of this section, I will use the word *acts* in all these ways. The book of Acts will serve as a viewfinder of sorts, one that helps us see the characteristics and qualities of the early faith that can guide and inspire our evangelism in the Inventive Age.

A PEOPLE MOVEMENT

Acts includes more than a hundred names—John, Philip, Simon, Peter, Paul, Sapphira, Stephen, Tabitha, Priscilla, to name just a few. This is the story of people, not just ideas or beliefs or even actions. It is about these particular people in particular places doing particular things. Their names are recorded because they matter to the story.

CHRISTIANITY HAS ALWAYS BEEN A FIRST-NAME FAITH.

These people were more than players in a story that had already been written. They were creating the story in real time, making it up as they went along. They didn't have a prescribed message they'd been taught and told to bring to others. They were living out what they understood to be the way of Jesus. And they had to live it out in every corner of the known world. What started as a Jewish movement in Jerusalem became a movement meant to be lived out by everyone, everywhere.

The book of Acts is the story of Jesus giving the apostles instructions. He says, "You will be my witnesses in Jerusalem, in all Judea and Samaria, and to the end of the earth."[22] That introduction to the story of Acts tells us that these people are more than messengers. They are witnesses. A witness doesn't give a generic report of events. A witness talks about what they know and have seen. That's our call as well—to bear witness to the ways God's story has connected with us and invite others to find connections of their own.

Acts can show us how to do just that. I'm going to use this chapter to work through Acts, treating it as a teaching tool for those of us seeking to be evangelists in the Inventive Age. It's a fairly long book, so I will engage with eight vignettes that I believe we evangelists can learn from. While these stories of the early followers obviously don't take into account the passion and fear types we have discussed, I think there are connecting points in these stories that resonate with each type.

RELEASE: ACTS 1

To understand the radical story playing out in Acts, we need some background information. The disciples had come from a culture in which the activity of God was supposedly centered in one place—the Temple in

Jerusalem. Actually, that's not quite accurate. It was not only in the Temple but in the Holy of Holies, the innermost room of the Temple. It was here that, each year, the high priest would approach the throne of God with an offering meant to bring forgiveness and blessing to the nation of Israel. Clearly, it was a very special place.

Because of that, the people allowed to enter the Temple had to be special too. Rules governed who could and couldn't enter—no one considered unclean, no one who was disabled or ill, no servants, no women, no children, and most certainly no Gentiles. There was no all-access pass unless you were one of the highest religious figures in the land.

The disciples met in the Temple's outer colonnade, the only place Gentiles were permitted to gather. This area is referred to as Solomon's Porch (named after King David's son Solomon, who constructed the Temple) and is the inspiration for the name of my church—we liked the idea of a place where everyone could meet.

There were clear distinctions between those who were allowed to approach the holiness of God and those who weren't. But Jesus changed that. He didn't come to transfer the power from the Temple to the church. He came to do away with power and privilege altogether.

Acts, then, starts off with a call to carry the story of Jesus far from the walls of the Temple, even to places no good Jew would ever go. Perhaps sometimes we don't think much about the details of Jesus' words to his disciples. But when he told them to spread the story from Jerusalem into the countryside of Samaria, they had to recalibrate everything they thought they knew.

Samaria was a region filled with people who, hundreds of years earlier, married themselves off to the Assyrians as a way to end a war. As a result, they developed a

form of Abrahamic faith that connected them to the promise of Abraham but not the way of Moses, David, or Solomon. Their faith was not Temple-focused, and therefore it
was an abomination to many Jews.

It wasn't just the disciples listening to Jesus who
would have been uncomfortable with heading to Samaria;
the Samaritans wouldn't have been thrilled about their
arrival. In the story of Jesus and the Samaritan woman at
the well, the woman is acutely aware of the friction between her and this Jewish man. She says, "'Why do you, a
Jewish man, ask for something to drink from me, a Samaritan woman?' (Jews and Samaritans didn't associate with
each other.)"[23]

After Jesus explains that he knows all about her
situation, she responds, "Sir, I see that you are a prophet.
Our ancestors worshipped on this mountain, but you and
your people say that it is necessary to worship in Jerusalem."[24]

When Jesus called his followers to witness in Samaria, it meant they had to see Samaritans as part of the
story of God, just like Jesus did.

All through the story of Acts, the disciples were discovering, to borrow a phrase from Peter, that "God doesn't
show partiality."[25]

One of the hardest adjustments for any of us to
make is to ferret out our own favoritism. It is one thing to
acknowledge that God accepts all people, but to do the
same ourselves is even more difficult. But in the Inventive
Age, an age of global influence, post-traditional thinking,
and particular people, evangelism begins with finding the
truth in all places, not just a select few. It means not allowing anyone to take the unique role of God's messenger or
God's activity. It means unleashing the gospel and paying attention to Jesus when he says: "God's Spirit blows

wherever it wishes. You hear its sound, but you don't know where it comes from or where it is going."[26]

INVITE: ACTS 2

In the Inventive Age, there is no shortage of stories meant to explain who we are and what our purpose is. For some of us, this is thrilling—it means there are countless ways to connect the story of God with the stories people are already telling. But for others, this is terrifying—it means there are countless ways the story of God can be misconstrued and misused.

Acts tells of a similar situation. Chapter 2 starts off with a strange and wonderful event:

> When Pentecost Day arrived, they were all to-gether in one place. Suddenly a sound from heaven like the howling of a fierce wind filled the entire house where they were sitting. They saw what seemed to be individual flames of fire alighting on each one of them. They were all filled with the Holy Spirit and began to speak in other languages as the Spirit enabled them to speak. There were pious Jews from every na-tion under heaven living in Jerusalem. When they heard this sound, a crowd gathered. They were mystified because everyone heard them speaking in their native languages. They were surprised and amazed, saying, "Look, aren't all the people who are speaking Galileans, every one of them? How then can each of us hear them speaking in our native language?"[27]

Pentecost was a Jewish holiday that was connected with Moses' journey up Mount Sinai, where he received the Commandments that became the foundation of God's covenant with the nation of Israel. It's a dramatic story filled with wind, fire, smoke, and the voice of God. It's a story of waiting and wondering and watching in awe:

When morning dawned on the third day, there
was thunder, lightning, and a thick cloud on the
mountain, and a very loud blast of a horn. All
the people in the camp shook with fear. Moses
brought the people out of the camp to meet
God, and they took their place at the foot of the
mountain. Mount Sinai was all in smoke because
the LORD had come down on it with lightning.
The smoke went up like the smoke of a hot fur-
nace, while the whole mountain shook violently.
The blasts of the horn grew louder and louder.
Moses would speak, and God would answer him
with thunder.[28]

Here's a bit of the non-identical repetition I men-
tioned earlier. The Acts Pentecost story echoes the original
Pentecost story. Like the Israelites, the apostles were trying to live the story of God's promise of release from op-
pression. They were seeking the freedom to be the blessing of God in all the world.

When the book of Acts tells of the disciples being
sent to wait in Jerusalem, the similarity starts to show.
The people are gathered, the wind starts to blow, people
are celebrating, there is waiting, there is wind, and there
is fire of that first Pentecost. But in this case, it wasn't
one person heading to the mountain on behalf of the
community. They were all upstairs. It wasn't one person
speaking for God but all of them speaking in every
language. The days of making a pilgrimage to Jerusalem
as they did for the Pentecost celebration in Acts were
over. With this new page in the story, people could form
Pentecost communities all over the world. The story
expanded and continued on.

The placement of this narrative in the story of the
Acts of the Apostles suggests that there's something important about telling the story of God in every language.
And since language is not only the words we use but the
way we think, which is influenced by the way we live, this
story creates entirely new avenues upon which the story

of God might travel. It means that evangelism has to be multilingual. We are called to tell the story as a continuation of the stories people are already living.

This invitation asks us to participate in the Pentecost activity of telling and hearing the story of God in all languages. It's interesting that in the Acts story it's not the content of what was said that amazed those who heard it. We are not even given the transcript of what people said to one another. It was the fact that each person heard something that resonated. It was the language connection that caused them to be "surprised and bewildered."[29]

We must find ways to hear all the languages in our communities and our friendships. This is where the varied temperaments and personalities come into play. When we speak and listen in the language of others, we follow the Pentecost model of evangelism.

This takes some practice, because what we communicate and what people hear aren't always the same thing.

In 1988 I was a member of a basketball team that played in an international tournament in Nicaragua. The team was part of an effort to place high-level basketball teams made up of Christians in settings where they would compete with national teams from other countries. It was a way to develop friendships and do Christian ministry.

The organization's leaders had developed a long-term ministry in which they entered into partnerships with the groups organizing the tournaments and teams. There was also a desire for short-term ministry, so we players were encouraged to talk with our opponents about our faith.

The whole thing was built around the model of

conversational evangelism. As players we were asked to make connections with those other players and see if the conversation would lead to talking about God.

I don't know how effective that ministry was, but I know it changed me.

I remember one conversation with members of the Soviet Union team. Keep in mind that this was 1988. The Berlin Wall was still standing and communism was still going strong—or at least we thought so. We were still wary of those Soviets—we'd seen them try to take out James Bond. We'd seen Rocky Balboa get pummeled by Ivan Drago in *Rocky IV* and cheered when "we" fought back. We'd heard stories from our parents about hiding under their school desks during bomb drills and the basement bomb shelters meant to protect them from the nuclear weapons the Soviets had aimed at our shores.

The members of the Soviet team in our tournament had never met nor talked with Americans, and my teammates and I had never talked with a communist. We were nervous and excited to meet one another.

The day before we were to play the Soviets, our team set up a meeting with their team to exchange customary gifts and, we hoped, start friendships that would lead to conversations about faith. We offered our gifts to one another and, with the occasional help of translators, we talked about our lives in America and the Soviet Union. We talked about family. And we talked about God.

I felt a wonderful connection with one of the players, Anatoly. We were about the same age and were both recently married, unlike most of our teammates. He had heard very little about Christianity or God. This was another connection point for us, since up until 1983 I didn't know anything about God either. Like me, Anatoly had thought a lot about the idea of God but hadn't had anyone with whom he could share those thoughts. So we talked for hours.

We talked about God's care for us and God's love for us. Anatoly explained that he'd never thought about God that way. He was more of a scientist. He thought of God as a creator but not so much as a lover. I wanted to share the idea that God's love for us is a sign that God is intimately involved in our lives.

So I said, "Anatoly, do you love your wife?"

"Well, yes, I do," he said with his rich Russian accent and careful English.

Then he added, proudly, "Two, maybe three time a week."

All the Americans in the room burst out laughing. In the midst of my laughter, I said, "Really? Well, good for you!"

After we settled down, I tried to shift Anatoly's understanding from "making love to your wife" to "loving your wife." Then I tried to make the shift from Anatoly loving his wife to being loved by God, and from loving God to loving one another. But with my limited language options, those subtle shifts were far too complicated to explain.

I'm not sure Anatoly understood what I was saying, but something in *me* started to change. I wondered if I was talking about love as an abstract idea, a means to a greater end—Anatoly's conversion—or if I was acting out of pure friendship and a genuine desire to connect with Anatoly.

I really did like him. We were of similar age and life stage. We had grown up in different places but were very much alike. And this was an amazing experience for both of us, having grown up thinking of the other as the ultimate enemy and now sitting in a room together, enjoying each other and caring for each other. I think we both sensed the similarity in our experiences with God as well—that God was not the enemy who would battle us until we changed, but the stranger we were hoping to meet and expecting to love.

If there was any conversion at that meeting, it was in me. I realized how easy it was to talk about love without living in it. Our meeting was beneficial not because I could get him to understand a concept of love, but because we had put behind us the animosity that our countries had spent decades building up and replaced it with true friendship.

What became clear to me was that the language and the categories we thought would limit our connection became irrelevant when we started talking about the ways our lives connected with the story of God.

Our stories are already multilingual. We share passions and fears with people all over the world. The human experience transcends borders and linguistics. Like the fire and the wind and the voice of God, the story of God can find a resting place anywhere and everywhere.

INCLUDE: ACTS 3, 6

In Acts 3 the story is told of a beggar who was sitting outside the temple, asking for Peter to do something for him. This man, due to his physical disability, was not allowed to be in the Temple. Peter wrapped the story of Jesus around this man and made him part of the story:

> Meanwhile, a man crippled since birth was being carried in. Every day, people would place him at the temple gate known as the Beautiful Gate so

he could ask for money from those entering the
temple. When he saw Peter and John about to
enter, he began to ask them for a gift. Peter and
John stared at him. Peter said, "Look at us!"
So the man gazed at them, expecting to receive
something from them. Peter said, "I don't have
any money, but I will give you what I do have.
In the name of Jesus Christ the Nazarene, rise
up and walk!" Then he grasped the man's right
hand and raised him up. At once his feet and
ankles became strong. Jumping up, he began to
walk around. He entered the temple with them,
walking, leaping, and praising God. All the people
saw him walking and praising God. They recognized him as the same one who used to sit at the
temple's Beautiful Gate asking for money. They
were filled with amazement and surprise at what
had happened to him.[30]

Peter wasn't running a complex outreach program
for the lame-beggar community. He was simply responding in the rhythm of what was happening that day. Peter
was a frequent visitor to the Temple. In fact, he had been
there with Jesus just months earlier. The lame man was a
regular beggar at the gate, and Peter had almost certainly
walked by the man before. Why this time did they engage
each other? Why did Peter do what he did that day? Why
had Jesus not healed the man in his visits to the Temple?
The story doesn't answer these questions, but it does
tell us that the man engaged Peter and that initiated the
healing—another moment of non-identical repetition that
reminds us of Jesus and the many times he healed those
who engaged him.

This is a story of responding to the man who was
sitting on the outside of a system that did not bring meaning to his life. Peter takes the man by the hand and makes
him part of the story. This is our call in the Inventive Age.
We are to do more than talk about how we fit in the story.
We are to translate the story in such a way that others are
invited in.

EMBRACE: ACTS 4

The deeper we move into the book of Acts, the more we see the true expansiveness of God's story. The story starts in Jerusalem and ends in Rome, the center of the empire that for most of the characters in the story and early readers represented the extent of the world. The story kicks off with a small group hiding in a room, then carries on to extend to all of humanity. And this story that feels so immediate keeps pointing itself to the long, rich history of what came before it. Acts shows us that there is no end to the ways people can connect to the story of God.

In chapter 4, Peter is arrested by Temple officials for healing the beggar. Peter is asked to explain himself, to justify violating the rules of the Temple so blatantly. His response is indicative of the historical, expansive, and extending story he has hitched himself to:

> Then Peter, inspired by the Holy Spirit, answered, "Leaders of the people and elders, are we being examined today because something good was done for a sick person, a good deed that healed him? If so, then you and all the people of Israel need to know that this man stands healthy before you because of the name of Jesus Christ the Nazarene—whom you crucified but whom God raised from the dead. This Jesus is the stone you builders rejected; he has become the cornerstone! Salvation can be found in no one else. Throughout the whole world, no other name has been given among humans through which we must be saved."[31]

Peter speaks of this "good deed" in the context of what Jesus had done. In another case of non-identical repetition, we are reminded of Jesus being questioned by these same leaders for healing a lame man on the Sabbath in Mark 3:1-6.

Peter then connects Jesus back into the Old Testament by using a prophetic phrase from Psalm 118 about Jesus as the stone the builders rejected. It's as though Peter is reminding his accusers of the story they have been living, and letting them know that it is still playing out and extending far beyond their control.

Then Peter throws the door open even wider by saying this story belongs not only to those under the Temple structure or even to the Jews, but to everything that exists in the world. Some see the phrase "no other name has been given among humans through which we must be saved" as limiting or restricting the scope of Jesus' story, but Peter uses it to extend the story to everything under heaven. Everything.

We are all able to follow Peter's lead and tell a more expansive version of the story of God. Peter might be the "rock," but he was just an ordinary guy. Acts tells us, "The council was caught by surprise by the confidence with which Peter and John spoke. After all, they understood that these apostles were uneducated and inexperienced. They also recognized that they had been followers of Jesus."[32] See? Nothing special. Just two guys who understood that their story extended far behind them and the place where they now stood.

During the summer months at Solomon's Porch, we invite people to give what we call "soapbox sermons." Anyone in our community can sign up to give a sermon on anything they wish. I don't monitor those sermons or help put them together. They are reflections of the life of God living in the people of our community.

One night Ben shared an image that I think captures the notion of the extending story. This image, created by a Lutheran pastor named Chris Harrison as part of his Ph.D. work, gives us a different way of seeing all the verses of the Bible and how they connect with one another.

In Chris's words, he sought to "find an elegant solution to render the data, more than 63,000 cross-references. The bar graph that runs along the bottom of the chart below represents all of the chapters in the Bible. Books alternate in color between white and light gray. The length of each bar denotes the number of verses in the chapter. Each of the 63,779 cross-references found in the Bible is depicted by a single arc—the color corresponds to the distance between any two chapters, creating a rainbow-like effect."[33]

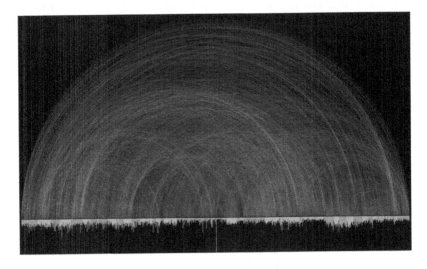

I think this is a great way to visualize the interplay between the stories in the Bible. While there is forward progression to the narrative—represented by the bar graph at the bottom—the story itself is interconnected and repeating.

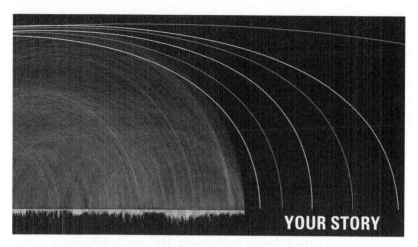

YOUR STORY

Ben, on his soapbox, was pointing to the same in the Acts of the Apostles, that the story of God's work does not end with the right side of the arc but keeps going in our world. Ben reminded us that the beauty of the story is that we are living in the next "act of the play" and that we too are living the story of what God is creating.

EVANGELISM IS CONNECTING THE STORY THAT WAS TO WHAT IS AND WHAT WILL BE.

WELCOME: ACTS 9

The Bible uses some twenty-six hundred names as it shows us the activity of God; there's no way to tell the story of God without telling the story of the people who participated with God. It's also the story of those who joined reluctantly. Moses wanted someone else to be the spokesperson. Sarah thought she could not have a child. Jonah wished for the destruction of Nineveh. Judas sold out Jesus.

The Bible is the story of people who aren't always sure if they want to live in harmony with the story of God. And it's the story of people who don't know they're invited.

The most well-known of these stories is that of Paul. Acts records Paul—back when he was Saul—as being the guy responsible for the execution of Stephen and threatening other Jesus followers. He was a Pharisee who was sent to bring an end to the community of Jesus-following Jews. He was the big cheese, the one who knocked heads together and kept the peace. He was feared, reviled, and probably high on everyone's list of "enemies of the faith."

Then Paul was struck—literally—with a personal call from Jesus. He was invited to align his story with God's story. And having been struck blind and with little choice but to do what he was told, he accepted.

But this story isn't Paul's alone. It's also the story of a disciple named Ananias. Even though he was already a follower of Jesus, he too was called out and invited into the story in a new way. Here's how Acts tells it:

In Damascus there was a certain disciple named Ananias. The Lord spoke to him in a vision, "Ananias!" He answered, "Yes, Lord." The Lord instructed him, "Go to Judas' house on Straight Street and ask for a man from Tarsus named Saul. He is praying. In a vision he has seen a man named Ananias enter and put his hands on him to restore his sight." Ananias countered, "Lord, I have heard many reports about this man. People say he has done horrible things to your holy

people in Jerusalem. He's here with authority
from the chief priests to arrest everyone who
calls on your name." The Lord replied, "Go! This
man is the agent I have chosen to carry my name
before Gentiles, kings, and Israelites. I will show
him how much he must suffer for the sake of my
name." Ananias went to the house. He placed
his hands on Saul and said, "Brother Saul, the
Lord sent me—Jesus, who appeared to you on
the way as you were coming here. He sent me
so that you could see again and be filled with
the Holy Spirit." Instantly, flakes fell from Saul's
eyes and he could see again. He got up and was
baptized. After eating, he regained his strength.
He stayed with the disciples in Damascus for
several days.[34]

Ananias was reluctant to go; Paul was reluctant to
go. But the invitation was offered just the same.

Evangelism is not and never has been some onto-
logical change that takes place in the heavenly realms. It is
an existential change *in people* living with real fears and
passions. Paul had to have the flakes fall from his eyes so
he could see that the one he had been seeking to destroy
was the one who saved him. And Ananias had to open his
home to the one from whom he was hiding.

When we think about evangelism as something
that offers a change of circumstance, we can extend the
freedom to allow each person to accept the invitation on
her own terms. Paul didn't eat, drink, or see anything for
three days. Ananias had to call the one who was hateful
his brother. This is no easy transition.

As a pastor, I often have conversations in which
people are fairly open about their doubts and unbelief. I
know some pastors feel a lot of anxiety about these conversations—there's a lot of pressure to "fix" these people
and make sure they don't wander too far from the fold.

But it's one of my favorite parts of the job. I really like being invited into the realities of people's lives, especially into their places of doubt. There is just no better place to *be* our faith than in the unsteady balance between belief and unbelief.

My friend Tony helped me understand the importance of this mix when he pointed out a story in the Gospel of Mark. The story involves a father who has brought his son to the disciples to see if they could free the boy from an epilepsy-like condition. Unable to help the boy, the disciples began to argue. Just then, the boy went into a convulsion in front of Jesus. Mark tells the rest of the story:

> Jesus asked [the boy's] father, "How long has this been going on?" He said, "Since he was a child. It has often thrown him into a fire or into water trying to kill him. If you can do anything, help us! Show us compassion!" Jesus said to him, "'If you can do anything'? All things are possible for the one who has faith." At that the boy's father cried out, "I have faith; help my lack of faith!"[35]

The mix of belief and unbelief. Believing, but also knowing that we need to overcome our unbelief. What a wonderful place to be! This isn't a paradox or a problem to be solved. It is the richness of an honest life.

While I find this to be the wonderful territory of healthy faith, others have a much harder time dealing with their unbelief. It feels so much more powerful than their belief. Others want to keep building their belief even in the midst of unbelief.

Awhile ago I received an e-mail from a college student who was interested in our church but had lots of questions. She was attending a Christian college that places heavy emphasis on having certainty about your faith. And she was having a hard time finding that certainty.

She wrote:

> Hi Doug,
>
> I'm interested in attending Solomon's Porch. I have come to visit twice before and have really liked it. I was wondering if there are a lot of students from my college who attend the church. As a current student, I am unsure of Christianity and question whether or not Solomon's Porch is a place for me to explore my spirituality without the pressure of having to be the typical Christian college student—the one who pretends to have it all together. I have nothing together and I'm unsure of everything.
>
> Kati
>
> Don't believe everything you think

Her situation is so familiar and so inspiring. She is looking for a community in which she can live a mix of belief and unbelief. She knows she has doubts, and she's okay with that. At the same time, she wants to find a place where she can explore and grow. She wasn't looking outside her faith for ways to explore her belief; she was looking for a way forward that did not force her to pretend to be something she wasn't.

I read her e-mail and thought of the father talking to Jesus—I do believe. Help me with my unbelief.

I was also intrigued by her standard e-mail salutation: "Don't believe everything you think." I got the sense she was able to look even at her own thoughts as having the potential to be part of both her belief and her unbelief. She's not being ironic; she is being honest. She knows, at some level, what we all need to know, that the most trust-worthy beliefs are those that are always in the process of change.

In many ways Kati is right where so many of us are—unbelieving believers or believing unbelievers.

With so many of us in this situation, inviting others to take on our faith is a sticky proposition. Why would we call people to a state of mixture? It seems better to wait until we are set in our faith so others can avoid the trouble we've experienced.

For many of us, the good news is that we don't have a settled system, that our belief can shift and grow and change. What we see in the story of the conversion of Paul was that he went from certainty to belief. He was confident in his earlier convictions, so much so that he was willing to kill for them. But then he was called to a bigger story, a more complete story, a more open story. Paul becomes the apostle not of a dogma but of the living Spirit of God that will come upon all people and call them to be people of active faith.

LISTEN: ACTS 10, 11

I used to think of the Bible as monocultural. In my mind, all the stories took place in the same basic area and involved people who were ethnically and religiously simi-lar to one another. But Acts tells a much better story.

In Acts, we find people in small communities where there were just a handful of Jesus followers and people sharing the story of God in large cosmopolitan centers. Far from being monocultural, this society was made up of complex interactions between various social, religious, and ethnic groups. That complexity is the current that flows all the way through the book of Acts.

This cross-cultural engagement was particularly complicated when it came to the interactions between ceremonially clean Jews and Gentiles.

The early Christians were radically committed to telling a story that fit the people, no matter who those people were. But this wasn't just about heading to Samaria to share the story with the "enemy." Their commitment extended beyond what the disciples considered their religious boundaries, too. It was one thing to reshape the contours of the Jewish faith in light of Jesus. It was another thing altogether to allow Gentiles to participate in that faith.

The major theological debate of the first century of Christianity was centered on the Gentile problem. The question: Did non-Jews need to convert and become culturally Jewish to be part of the work God was doing through Jesus? Gentiles had long been invited to convert to Jewish life. The early disciples continued that expectation for Gentiles who wanted to follow Jesus.

The issue was so important during the first twenty-five years of the Jesus community that many of the theological conversations and writings of the day centered on this question. Many of the apostle Paul's letters deal specifically with this issue—Romans is almost entirely a treatise on this argument.

In Acts we learn that after much debate—including a special meeting of the Jewish elders—the answer to the question was a resounding "No!" The desire to welcome the outsider has been part of the Christian faith ever since. But it didn't come easily.

Tucked into the record of the Acts of the Apostles is the fascinating story of Peter and Cornelius. It's one of the few places in Acts where the pace slows a bit and the author spends two whole chapters telling one story in great detail. It's a signal to the reader that this story is vitally important. It serves to illustrate just how difficult it was for both Jews and Gentiles to overcome their prejudices against each other and find a common path of faith.

It's helpful to know that Peter wasn't just any disciple. He was a Jew's Jew, a man so committed to the laws of Judaism that he would not even talk to non-Jews, lest he be made unclean. The original readers of Acts would have known that about Peter, a background that would make an already powerful story even more meaningful to them.

The story starts with a man named Cornelius. We're told he's a devout, godly man. He is also a leader in the Roman military that was occupying Jerusalem and the surrounding area—the same Roman military that had put Jesus to death. One afternoon, Cornelius has a strange encounter with an angel—recall the connection between angels and evangelism—who tells him to go find a guy named Peter. The angel even tells Cornelius where to find this Peter. What he doesn't tell him is why. But Cornelius follows the angel's call and sends his workers to go find Peter.

Meanwhile, Peter is having a strange encounter of his own. He's hungry, waiting for lunch to be served, and is deep in the midst of one of his customary three-times-a-day prayer sessions when he has a vision of four-footed animals, reptiles, and birds—all of them specifically forbidden for a ceremonially clean man to touch, according to Jewish law. In the vision, the voice of the Lord tells Peter to kill and eat the creatures. Peter says, "Absolutely not, Lord! I have never eaten anything impure or unclean."[36]

The voice spoke to him a second time, "Never consider unclean what God has made pure."[37] This whole vision/conversation ordeal happens three times (Peter + denying something three times = non-identical repetition) before Peter snaps back to reality and wonders what on earth that was all about.

Suddenly there's a knock at the door. Peter opens it to find three Roman soldiers who have come to take him to see Cornelius. Despite what I imagine was his first response—Yeah, right. I'm going to enter the home of a Roman centurion, the kind of guy who killed Jesus—Peter agrees to go with them after they explain that the Lord told Cornelius to send for him. Not only does Peter agree to go with them, he invites them into his house. Peter, the Jew, invited Roman soldiers into his house. He welcomed his oppressors.

I doubt that this was easy for Peter. Just as he followed the dietary laws of his Jewish faith, he followed the laws that forbade him from consorting with Gentiles. Peter had spent his entire life keeping this religious commitment. How could God possibly be calling him to leave those commitments for a new faithfulness? To add salt to the wound, all this was happening in Caesarea, a city named for the Caesar, who required everyone to worship him as the son of God.

Peter, the great apostle, invites Roman soldiers into the house because they told him they had a message from God. I would imagine that without the story of his own vision still alive inside him, Peter never would have gone along with this request. But the story of God had intersected with Peter's own story in a stunning way.

So Peter goes with the men and enters the house of Cornelius. Upon Peter's arrival, Cornelius "fell at his feet in order to honor him."[38] And Peter, one of Jesus' closest friends, one of the leaders of the new movement, says to this Gentile, "Get up! Like you, I'm just a human."[39]

Peter then calls out this strange situation for what it is—the meeting of people who have never stood together in the same room, much less had a conversation—when he meets the people who have gathered at the house. He says, "You all realize that it is forbidden for a Jew to associate or visit with outsiders. However, God has shown me that I should never call a person impure or unclean. For this reason, when you sent for me, I came without objection. I want to know, then, why you sent for me."[40] Peter had to change in order to participate with what God was leading him into.

He continues to point to his change of heart by saying, "I really am learning that God doesn't show partiality to one group of people over another. Rather, in every nation, whoever worships him and does what is right is acceptable to him. This is the message of peace he sent to the Israelites by proclaiming the good news through Jesus Christ: He is Lord of all!"[41]

The story builds as Peter proclaims the story of Jesus and the people in Cornelius's house have their own non-identical repetition of Pentecost. At this Peter includes the entire household in the community of faith by saying, "These people have received the Holy Spirit just as we have. Surely no one can stop them from being baptized with water, can they?"[42]

Any walls between Jews and Gentiles that might have existed for Peter crumbled to the ground. This declaration—that all are invited into the story of Jesus—was revolutionary, not just for Cornelius, but for Peter too. Both men listened to the call God placed in them.

BOTH OF THEM HAD TO OVERCOME THEIR IDEAS ABOUT THE OTHER.

That is the beauty of evangelism—both people are changed by their involvement in the life of the other.

The reason this story takes two chapters is that this event—the Gentiles receiving the word of God—did not go over well with Peter's fellow Christ followers. So Peter tells them the whole story. And he changes their minds.

The same story that was powerful for the Gentiles was powerful to those who opposed the Gentiles.

As we transition into the Inventive Age, we will experience some growing pains. Among them is this lingering pressure to keep the faith pure by being sure the righteous stay away from the unclean. There are Christians who are stuck in the Information Age mentality that right belief trumps everything else and that we can't risk sullying the purity of Truth by exposing it to those who might claim some other truth.

That's not so different from the culture that was thriving in the first century of the Christian faith. The first followers had to make sense of the world where faith belonged to the elite, not the common person. There was an intentionally narrow path, and that meant not everyone would fit. The common and the holy were to remain separate, lest the common infect the holy. For the first Christian evangelists, the shift from the faith being holy to the people being holy was profound.

The Inventive Age is blurring the boundaries we once used to tell us who was "us" and who was "them." We live where we want to live, not where our tribe or ancestors lived. We have access to information on people close to us and people on the other side of the ideological, political, theological, and global spectrums. All of that makes it harder for us to have clear divides between groups of people. And while that can be frustrating to

those who define themselves by these divisions, for those
of us eager to tell the story of God in the Inventive Age, it's
a wonderful development.

PROCLAIM: ACTS 15

The issue of Gentiles being included in the story of
God through Jesus was so significant in the first century
that the early church created entire structures to discuss it.
One of these structures is described in Acts.

Because Jerusalem was the center of the Jesus
community for the first few decades, a meeting was called
to decide if this new movement was going to tell the same
story on this matter.

Acts 15 opens with a story about a group of
people—powerful, well-educated, and well-positioned
leaders from among the Pharisees—who argued that
no one could be saved unless they were circumcised. In
Acts this group is referred to in some translations as "the
Circumcisers." This was not a fringe group or a radical
element within the community. No, these were the mucky
mucks. They knew the Law of Moses better than the
rest, and their desire to keep the custom of Moses alive
was not inessential or unimportant. This debate was not
about some tangential issue. People on both sides of the
discussion took it very seriously, for it sat at the heart of
the story of the community. When people heard about
Peter's weekend with Cornelius, it became clear that they
needed to get this figured out—and soon.

So the question became: Did a Gentile have to convert to Judaism in order to follow Jesus or not?

For a Gentile to be circumcised and keep the Law of
Moses would have been no simple process. It would have
meant a change in culture, community, and worldview. A

THE ACTS OF EVANGELISM

Gentile would need to make significant physical and social changes to join in with this new faith. For some, it would cost them their families, their livelihood, their friendships. It would unmoor them from every foundation in their lives.

There were those who had already done this—Acts refers to them as Gentile converts or circumcised believers. It might have been difficult, but they believed this was what God required. The Pharisees and those on their side felt strongly that they could not simply set aside the Law of Moses to accommodate the Gentiles. If they let go of one part of the law, wouldn't they eventually end up letting go of the whole thing? It was a legitimate fear and a legitimate question.

This kind of debate goes on all the time in our day. What does it mean to be a Christian? Can you drink alcohol? Swear? Do you have to read the Bible literally? Do you have to claim Jesus as your personal Savior? Do you have to be baptized as an infant? What exactly are the requirements of our faith? So we know how a debate like this can take on a life of its own.

Those arguing that Gentiles should not have to convert from one culture to another were themselves circumcised men. Paul, Peter, Barnabas, and the entire lot were either born Jews or had converted. So they weren't arguing for their own benefit or to justify their own situation. They were doing all they could to be sure the good news was actually good. They knew the benefit of being a circumcised Jew in the story of Jesus and weren't trying to invalidate that expression. But they also knew that Gentiles had experienced Jesus as well and had done so without such a conversion.

It was Peter who made the point, "God, who knows people's deepest thoughts and desires, confirmed this by giving them the Holy Spirit, just as he did to us. He made no distinction between us and them, but purified their deepest thoughts and desires through faith. Why then are you now challenging God by placing a burden on the shoulders of these disciples that neither we nor our ancestors could bear? On the contrary, we believe that we and they are saved in the same way, by the grace of the Lord Jesus."[43]

There was nothing good in a call that required leaving your culture in order to follow Jesus. It was too difficult to bear and not necessary.

In the Inventive Age, those who are told they can only see the story of God through someone else's lens often find themselves facing this same problem. They are being asked to change their root story, to resonate with someone else's tone. And it doesn't sit well with them.

As the debate continued, James, who may well have been a brother of Jesus, made his case, saying, "Therefore, I conclude that we shouldn't create problems

THOSE PRACTICING THE ACTS WANTED GOOD NEWS TO BE GOOD FOR THE HEARER.

for Gentiles who turn to God."[44]

The apostles' assumption was that the role of an evangelist is to tear down barriers that keep us from God, not add more of them. Everyone meets God as he or she is able, and there's nothing righteous about making it harder to do.

This needs to be the impulse of Inventive Age evangelism as well. Communities and individuals have to really listen to the way we tell God's story and ask ourselves if we are doing anything to make it harder for people to join in with that story.

After the opposing sides concluded their council meeting, they announced their decision in a letter that could be read to the Gentile communities:

> The apostles and the elders, to the Gentile brothers and sisters in Antioch, Syria, and Cilicia. Greetings! We've heard that some of our number have disturbed you with unsettling words we didn't authorize. We reached a united decision to select some delegates and send them to you along with our dear friends Barnabas and Paul. These people have devoted their lives to the name of our Lord Jesus Christ. Therefore, we are sending Judas and Silas. They will confirm what we have written. The Holy Spirit has led us to the decision that no burden should be placed on you other than these essentials: refuse food offered to idols, blood, the meat from strangled animals, and sexual immorality. You will do well to avoid such things. Farewell.[45]

This letter asks the Gentiles to follow a set of customs that would allow those who are keeping the Law of Moses to engage in community with them. The evangelists didn't want a divided church, where one group met at one time and place and the other met somewhere else. They wanted the Gentiles and those following the Law of Moses to join together in the synagogue meetings. This is not a story of Gentiles becoming Jews or of Jews becoming Gentiles. It is the story of both being—and even extending—the story of God for the other.

The good news of this story was not that the law

prevailed—which it did for the Jews—but that these followers of Jesus knew it was essential that the story of the
gospel be proclaimed as truly good news of inclusion, acceptance, and unity for all.

CREATE: ACTS 11, 17

As the story of God's work through Jesus spread
around the known world, new collections of people came
together, creating a complex dynamism. This faith that just
years earlier had been centered in the story of Israel and
located in Jerusalem was now the story of all people and
in such far-reaching places as Thessalonica, Berea, Am-
phipolis, and Apollonia. These were strange places with
a strange Greek culture. And yet there was resonance in
these places. Not only were they new places, they required
new allegiances. In these places "some were convinced
and joined Paul and Silas, including a larger number of
Greek God-worshippers and quite a few prominent wom-
en."[46]

Jews and Gentiles made strange partners. There
weren't many places where they could meet together without creating a cultural scene. Include women as prominent
leaders in the mix and you had something powerful happening. Acts was not only about people believing new
stories; it was about creating new places of belonging,
especially for those who had never belonged.

Jewish culture was patriarchal—men led in the Temple structure, men were the political leaders and property
owners. That was the custom and the theology. It was even
taught that this was how it was supposed to be, that the
created order was God over man and man over woman.

But among the evangelists, "there [was] neither
Jew nor Greek; there is neither slave nor free; nor is there
male and female, for you are all one in Christ Jesus."[47] The
issues of social structure were reorganized to make room

for everyone.

As you can imagine, this did not sit well with the religious establishment. Acts tells us they didn't know how to tamp down on this growing movement. They said, "'These people who have been disturbing the peace throughout the empire have also come here. What is more, Jason has welcomed them into his home. Every one of them does what is contrary to Caesar's decrees by naming someone else as king: Jesus.' This provoked the crowd and the city officials even more."[48]

The early evangelists were proclaiming a story in which the rules of the earthly kingdom were threatened, and those who benefited from those rules were desperate to hold on to them. Things aren't so different in the Inventive Age. As the world becomes more multicultural and our assumptions about power and authority change, those who benefit from holding on to their power have a vested interest in making sure the outsiders stay on the outside.

But like those first evangelists, we are called to create a world in which there is no ethnic or economic or gender division. We have to ask ourselves whom today's Jews and Gentiles, slaves and free, male and female might be. What barriers do we need to break down in order to be one in Christ Jesus?

And what will we create that serves to invite the outsider and include the outcast? The early church borrowed the system of meetings used by the Greeks for political gatherings—the *ecclesia*. Paul and the other apostles co-opted the idea as a starting point for the Gentile community. They didn't use the existing synagogues, but the ecclesia to call Gentiles into a community that claimed Jesus as their king. They took their cues from the culture in which they lived, not the religious structure that no longer had room for their expansive faith.

Evangelism in the Inventive Age, like evangelism in every age, will need to deal with the biases and discrimination of our day and time. As we proclaim good news, as we speak of the outcast being invited to full participation in the faith, we must also create the new structures that will hold all of the stories playing out among God's people.

SECTION 6

TO THE ENDS OF THE EARTH

Our culture is changing. It always has been and always will be. That constant change means that each time and place has particular challenges and opportunities for those of us seeking to proclaim good news.

In the Inventive Age, we are faced with an educated population who no longer need to be told what to think or what do to. Information is a cheap commodity and nearly everyone has access to it in one way or another. People are no longer bound to the limits of location or tradition, leaving us to put aside the assumptions that once allowed us to pigeonhole people as "us" and "them." The authority we once claimed by virtue of our education or our ordination or our vocation no longer holds up in our culture of shared power, flattened structures, and relational networks. In this age of self-awareness and personal empowerment, we do well to pay attention to the hopes and dreams and fears of the people we seek to evangelize.

It is, to be sure, a complicated time in which to proclaim good news. And I wouldn't want it any other way.

The gospel of Jesus has never been a generic message. The Christian gospel has never been at home on a three-page pamphlet or an illustrated tract. It is far too personal and yet far too expansive to be reduced to a formula or a system. The gospel we proclaim is about breaking free of the structures and powers that bind us. It is about opening ourselves up to the Spirit of God and allowing the story of God to resonate with our deepest passions and fears.

It will take time for us to follow in the way of the first apostles and figure out how to release and invite and include others in the story we are telling. It will take practice for us to learn how to welcome and listen and create in ways that are meaningful to others. But Peter and Paul and Silas and all the other people living out the Acts of the

Apostles showed us that true evangelism is never easy, especially for the evangelist.

N. T. Wright offers a compelling understanding of what it means to live out the story of God in the Inventive Age. He compares our calling to the missing fifth act of a Shakespearean drama. He writes:

> The first four acts provide, let us suppose, such a wealth of characterization, such a crescendo of excitement within the plot, that it is generally agreed that the play ought to be staged. Nevertheless, it felt inappropriate actually to write a fifth act once and for all: it would freeze the play into one form, and commit Shakespeare as it were to being prospectively responsible for work not in fact his own. Better, it might be felt, to give the key parts to highly trained, sensitive, and experienced Shakespearian actors who would immerse themselves in the first four acts, and in the language and culture of Shakespeare and his time, and who would then be told to work out a fifth act for themselves."[49]

In Wright's illustration, we are called to write the fifth act. We know the style of our playwright. We know the story that has come before. And now, like those first followers of Jesus, we are to take the story into our day and time and proclaim it as good news to each person we meet.

We are a sent people with a story to tell and a story we are living as well.

Go.

Go and be witnesses.

In your Jerusalem.

In your Judea and Samaria.

GO TO THE ENDS OF THE EARTH.

And then come back and change us all.

ABOUT THE AUTHOR

Doug Pagitt is the founder of Solomon's Porch, a holistic, missional Christian community in Minneapolis, Minnesota, and one of the pioneering leaders of Emergent Village, a social network of Christians around the world. He is also cofounder of an event and social media company and author of a number of groundbreaking books: *A Christianity Worth Believing, Church in the Inventive Age, Community in the Inventive Age,* and *Preaching in the Inventive Age.*

Doug can be reached at:

Twitter: @Pagitt

www.DougPagitt.com

www.facebook.com/DougPagittspage

www.SolomonsPorch.com

NOTES

SECTION 1

1. Luke 2:10

2. Isa. 52:7

3. Luke 1:1-4

4. John 20:30-31

SECTION 3

5. www.languagemonitor.com

6. www.christianity.about.com/od/denominations/p/christiantoday.htm

7. www.tyndalearchive.com/Scriptures/index.htm

8. http://commons.trincoll.edu/aris/

9. John 20:30-31

SECTION 4

10. Rom. 8:16

11. Rom. 12:5-8; 1 Cor. 12

12. For more detailed descriptions, go to enneagraminstitute.com.

13. NIV

14. www.enneagraminstitute.com

15. Gen. 3:8-10

16. Gen. 3:1-5

17. Gen. 4:3-8

18. www.enneagramspectrum.com

19. Christopher Chabris and Daniel Simons, *The Invisible Gorilla: And Other Ways Our Intuitions Deceive Us* (New York: Crown, 2010).

20. Ibid., 39.

21. Ibid., 16.

SECTION 5

22. Acts 1:8

23. John 4:9

24. John 4:19-20

25. Acts 10:34

26. John 3:8

27. Acts 2:1-8

28. Exod. 19:16-19

29. Acts 2:12

30. Acts 3:2-10

31. Acts 4:8-12

32. Acts 4:13

33. www.chrisharrison.net/index.php/

34. Acts 9:10-19

35. Mark 9:21-24

36. Acts 10:14

37. Acts 10:15

38. Acts 10:25

39. Acts: 10:26

40. Acts: 10:28-29

41. Acts 10:34-36

42. Acts 10:47

43. Acts 15:8-11

44. Acts 15:19

45. Acts 15:23-29

46. Acts 17:4

47. Gal. 3:28

48. Acts 17:6-8

SECTION 6

49. www.ntwrightpage.com/Wright_Bible_
    Authoritative.htm

CPSIA information can be obtained at www.ICGtesting.com
Printed in the USA
BVOW08s1536280614

357659BV00008B/195/P